# PARTICIPANT
# OBSERVATION

## COMMENTARY

"Havens has made a major contribution by putting forward one of the clearest formulations of a theory of Sullivanian technique. This book is not only an exposition of Sullivan's concepts as contrasted with classical psychoanalytic technique and the existential approach but a practical volume on how to work psychotherapeutically with the more severely ill patients who are more apt to use mechanisms as denial and projection as well as splitting."

Clarence G. Schulz, M.D.
Sheppard and Enoch Pratt Hospital
Baltimore, Maryland

"Leston Havens, in the conservative sanctuary of Boston Psychoanalysis and Harvard Medical School, has rediscovered Harry Stack Sullivan, and with great skill and clarity has accomplished the task, long spoken of, but heretofore never completed, of explicating Sullivan for the sophisticated dynamic clinical psychiatrist."

Maurice R. Green, M.D., P.C.
South Beach Psychiatric Center
Staten Island, New York

# PARTICIPANT OBSERVATION

## The Psychotherapy Schools in Action

LESTON HAVENS, M.D.

**JASON ARONSON INC.**
*Northvale, New Jersey • London*

**Library of Congress Cataloging-in-Publication Data**

ISBN: 1-56821-108-2
Library of Congress Catalog Number: 84-45109

Manufactured in the United States of America. Jason Aronson Inc. offers books and cassettes. For information and catalog write to Jason Aronson Inc., 230 Livingston Street, Northvale, New Jersey 07647.

# Preface

The pages that follow outline a therapeutic system gleaned from the writings and supervisory advice of Harry Stack Sullivan. I write "glean" because the field of Sullivan's work has already been gone over for its theoretical and diagnostic significance, leaving it bare enough now to show forth bits and pieces of technical advice. I have developed these into a systematic technique that can be called, in Sullivan's words, participant observation. There is, however, no way this can be understood until the other principal methods are developed in contrast. I therefore describe and enlarge psychoanalytic, existential, and behaviorist ways of working in the context of specific clincial examples. Hence this book's subtitle: The Psychotherapy Schools in Action.

Sullivan's own account of his working methods, *The Psychiatric Interview*, is a conglomerate of technical suggestions, like most descriptions of psychotherapy. It incorporates the objective-descriptive examination, free associative method, social service casework, and what interests us the most, his remarkable intuition. The basic tools of diagnostic or therapeutic power spring from the inventive gifts of remarkable individuals, whether Freud's associative method, Binswanger's understanding of the conditions of empathy, or Auenbrugger's ability to compare the percussion of his father's wine barrels to the percussion of the human chest. Sullivan gave his intuitive gift its fullest articulation in his theoretical writings, which he illustrated richly with anecdotes. What was unique in his actual working methods, however, remained largely unsystematized. Partly for this reason his technical suggestions strike many as idiosyncratic, even bizarre. I suspect they must have appeared to Sullivan himself as mysterious as intuitions typically are.

Sullivan's intuitions are striking precisely because they reflect an approach rational, coherent, sometimes compelling. Surely Freud's early intuitions and free associative method must also seem mysterious to anyone not familiar with his explanations. For his part, Sullivan did not provide technical explanations. It is therefore necessary to bring his clinical suggestions together, throw the light of his theoretical position on them and, most important, draw from them their vital principles. Then we may accord participant observation some of the respect as a systematic technique that we at present accord only to the objective-descriptive examination and psychoanalysis.

A grasp of this technology serves another, more pragmatic purpose than simply "discovering" how Sullivan may have worked. The great mixing of schools and school methods so characteristic of the contemporary psychiatric and psychological atmosphere leaves students bewildered. Today many psychoanalysts sound like existentialists. Several of the most recent movements combine analytic, interpersonal, and existential methods with a bravura which suggests that here is something absolutely new and original. Students shop at a market in which both names and merchandise change unpredictably! A systematic understanding of the tools of psychiatry can only help to clarify the essences of the major developments.

I have used material principally from four sources, *The Psychiatric Interview* (Sullivan, 1954), *Clinical Studies in Psychiatry* (Sullivan, 1956), White's account of Sullivan's treatment methods in the *Contributions* (ed., Mullahy, 1952), and the accounts of two cases Sullivan supervised, in the 1947 volume of *Psychiatry* (Sullivan, 1947; Tower, 1947; Cohen, 1947). The bits and pieces are scattered. Furthermore, Sullivan's technique, like Freud's, underwent development. Just as Freud had to leave behind the objective-descriptive methods of electrical treatment and hypnotism, Sullivan had to leave behind both the objective-descriptive examination and free associative interviewing. He moved toward conceptions strikingly contemporary: field theory, relativism, and behaviorism.

Like a field theorist, Sullivan considered the main area of observation to be the transactions that occur between people. To this most individual of men, individuality seemed largely a mirage, a changing point in a field of constantly interacting forces. And in keeping with these conceptions he believed there was no objective vantage point. Like Henry James and Albert Einstein, Sullivan could experience his data only from a particular viewpoint: the observer participated, and every observation was relative to the stance of the observer. Finally, he was a behaviorist. His emphasis was on learning and experience rather than on instincts and fantasy. Society, rather than anatomy, was destiny.

Sullivan also brought to psychiatry a fresh perspective which I call the fictive attitude: everything encountered clinically he assumed to be a fiction until proved a fact. The interview is at once a canvas on which patient and doctor paint their imaginative creations of the moment and a stage on which they play their roles. Only by dispelling the fictions can one arrive at the facts. And the first fiction to be dispelled is what Bion calls "the numbing feeling of reality," our easy surrender to the social fantasy system of the moment.[1]

Students of object relations theory will find much in his work to admire. He and Melanie Klein were the father and mother of those conceptions. The operational principles developed here will seem to some "object relations theory in action."

Chapter 1 ("Sullivan's Fine Disregard") presents a series of his clinical anecdotes with suggestions as to what they represent: its purpose is to set the stage. Chapters 2 and 3 ("The Other

---

1. A psychoanalyst describes his experience at certain moments in a group when he "feels he is being manipulated so as to be playing a part, no matter how difficult to recognize, in somebody else's fantasy. . . ." This alienation effect is insidious. We are all prone to be drawn into social phantasy systems with the loss of one's own identity in the process, and only in retrospect become aware that this has happened. Bion goes on: "I believe the ability to shake one's self out of the numbing feeling of reality that is concomitant of this state is the prime requisite of the analyst in the group. . . ." (Bion, 1955) (Laing, 1969)

People in the Room" and "Managing Conflict") expand these suggestions into principles of participant observation; these principles are tested in chapter 4 against case material that Sullivan himself supervised, while chapter 5 contains an interview in which the author applies the principles.

The next four chapters are essentially an outline of work in progress. I suggest categories of interventions to implement the principles and a number of points of contrast to the other principal schools.

The Appendix is the revised version of a paper given at the Boston Psychoanalytic Society and Institute. The purpose of this paper is to suggest indications for the use of the newer clinical methods—participant observation and existential method—in psychoanalysis and psychotherapy. I was especially interested in relating these methods to the work of Kohut and Kernberg.

Those who worked with Sullivan will have many quarrels with my account. Sullivan was far too able a therapist to be merely a Sullivanian. But my search here has been for principles.

I want to thank Helen Swick Perry for referring me to the cases in chapter 4 (and for her stewardship of Sullivan's work, which with Patrick Mullahy's has kept alive a central line of psychiatric development), Alice Tallmadge for her help in organizing the material presented here, many medical students and residents at the Massachusetts Mental Health Center, and, above all, Susan Miller-Havens for the exchanges of clinical experience within which many of these ideas developed.

# Contents

# ONE

# Sullivan's Fine Disregard

There is nothing I can conceive in the way of interpersonal action about which one could not be trained to be anxious, so that if such an action is foreseen one feels anxious, and if it occurs one's self-esteem is reduced. The realm of this congeries of tensions is the area of one's training for life at the hands of significant others, and of how much or little one has been able to synthesize out of these training experiences. (Sullivan, 1953, p. 371)

THE ANXIOUS MOMENT marks the point "at which something disjunctive, something that tends to pull away from the other fellow, has first appeared or has suddenly increased. It signals a change from relatively uncomplicated movement toward a presumptively common goal to a protecting of one's self-esteem, with a definite complicating of the interpersonal action" (p. 378).

The way the person protects himself in turn indicates his interpretation of the anxiety provoking situation. The Sullivan interviewer manages anxiety by noticing what this interpretation is and then employing tools to affect it. These involve timing, the expression of nonverbal attitudes (tone, affect, specific vocabulary, etc.), and the creation of a dialectic between the patient's supposed reality and a more factual reality (through transitional statements and those particular transitional statements I call counterprojective remarks). All demand a high degree of attention to the patient's words and the "meanings" which lie behind those words, an ability to bring these underlying strains to the front without provoking anxiety or resentment, and a nonjudgmental attitude which can support and assure the patient who may be brought to express, for the first time, extremely sensitive material.

That application demands most of all the therapist's acute understanding of his actual role in the dialogue with the patient, not someone apart, but an agent of dynamic, even potentially controlling effects on the patient's responses.

Sullivan's vignettes illustrate what Mary White (ed. Mullahy, 1952) called his "fine disregard" of the classical rules. He was scholar enough to know the rules but daredevil enough to break them.

> When the work is going well, I finally run a considerable risk by beginning to be unpleasant and demanding about the patient's horrible thoughts and terrors. I now begin to indicate my disrespect for these things. 'God help us, why must we have this hokum when we are doing useful work most of the time? I know something bothers you, but does it have to be disguised as a catastrophe? These horrible thoughts, do they bring out goose pimples on you? If I remember anything horrible, I expect goose pimples.' (ed. Mullahy, 1952, p. 146)

Ostensibly, Sullivan is being disrespectful of the patient. Certainly he is being disrespectful of the material. The tone is mocking, sarcastic, and offhand; yet the patient may be relieved by this very nonchalance. Plainly Sullivan is not horrified.

If I hear some kind of involved business about homosexuality or abattoir fantasies of slashing and tearing,
I can surmise these things represent fantasies from an
early time when one had completely to inhibit the expression of rage. Kids find it easy to entertain fantasies
of taking the axe to troublesome parents and teachers
and making a slaughterhouse. One has to be prepared
for the eruption of this sort of thing, and probably my
response would be, 'Well, hell, you must have felt terribly **sore** sometimes in the past.' That proves that I
am not horrified and I don't get in too deep. I have
tossed out a lifeline, the awful stuff is before us, and
we are still there. (p. 147)

"Well, hell, you must have felt terribly sore sometimes in the
past." Now the tone is serious, but again undisturbed. The
"hell" is almost "so what," but more emphatic, and also a link
to the "terribly sore." Affects are being freely used, the doctor is
confident, but not at all "professional." And something about
the patient's affect is also conveyed: he must have been sore.
The patient may not allow himself to accept that, but not now
because he has reason to fear the therapist's disapproval of his
anger. Sullivan has done something better than saying "I am not
one of those who disapproves." He has shown he does not dis-
approve. He has abandoned the parental authoritative position
doctors so easily assume. We glimpse already one principle of
this technique. It is counterprojective: the patient's surmises
about the therapist's attitudes, his projections onto the therapist, are actively combatted.

Any word in Sullivan's statement could have been stressed,
for example, "sometimes" rather than "sore." Attention would
then be drawn away from the affect and toward a temporal
consideration; still greater permission would be given the patient's anger by slipping in, one might say, the mention of it and
also contradicting any idea the patient could have that the therapist thought he was *always* angry. Who has not the right to be

sometimes angry? Such a change of emphasis might be necessary if the patient's anger were still more deeply forbidden. On
the other hand, if his anger were less forbidden, the affect could
be reemphasized, as by stressing "felt," "terribly," *and* "sore"—
successive invitations to explore the affect. With this technique,
words are used like notes in music, to play upon the mind.

Not only are the therapist's tones important, so are the patient's. This is an ear-to-ear method.

> If somebody is attempting to tell you what the busi-
> ness of a journeyman electrician is, things may go on
> quite well until he is on the verge of saying something
> about the job which pertains to a field in which he has
> been guilty of gross disloyalty to his union, at which
> time his voice will sound altered. He may still give you
> the facts about what his journeyman electrician should
> be and do, but he will sound different in the telling. A
> great part of the experience which one slowly gains
> takes the form of showing mild interest in this point at
> which there is a tonal difference. Thus one would per-
> haps say, 'Oh yes, and the payment of two percent of
> one's income to this fund for the sick and wounded is
> almost never neglected by good union members, I
> gather'; to which the other might reply, again sound-
> ing quite different from what he had earlier, 'Exactly.
> It's a very important part of membership.' And then,
> if you feel quite sure of the situation, you might say,
> 'And one, of course, which you have never violated.'
> Whereupon the other person sounds very different,
> indeed; perhaps quite indignant, and says, 'Of course
> not!' If you are extremely sure of the way things go, you
> might even say, 'Well, of course you understand that
> I have no suspicion about you, but your voice sound-
> ed odd when you mentioned it, and I couldn't help
> wondering if it were preying on your mind.' At this
> he may sound still more different, and say, 'Well, as a
> matter of fact, early in my journeymanship I actually
> did pocket a little of the percentage, and it has been on

> my conscience ever since.' And the business moves
> along. (p. 123-124)

"Oh yes, and the payment of two percent of one's income to this fund for the sick and wounded is almost never neglected by good union members, I gather." Now Sullivan speaks for the patient's conscience. He is trying to hide, for a moment, his suspicions of the patient. He knows he cannot hide in silence; that silence will fill up, as it were, with the patient's uneasy conviction of being suspected. Sullivan is temporarily supporting the patient's game.

Note how far he goes. "And one, of course, which you have never violated," inviting the vociferous and no doubt increasingly hollow "Of course not." The patient is being drawn further and further out on a limb. Paradoxically this makes possible his confession.

The patient is able to confess because Sullivan has first established himself as vociferously unsuspicious. By drawing out the patient's increasingly hollow denials he has also put the patient in a more and more uncomfortable position. He has increased the gap between truth and statement to the point where the patient is relieved to narrow it again. I call this widening and balancing. Opposing parts of a conflict are each given expression, one after the other, both the electrician's prohibition against cheating and whatever led him to cheat. We will see that the purpose of this is not insight; that might only embarrass the patient. The purpose is to learn new responses through perceiving the social field differently. We will also see that the tool of this social learning is what Sullivan called transitional statements.

Here is a variation on the same theme.

> Let us suppose the patient says, 'Doctor, I am a homo-
> sexual.' What do you do then? You can hear what is
> said. You can presume it does not mean what you
> think. You can notice it is extremely important to the

patient and you can say something which indicates
you have survived the blow, that you don't think it is
as awful as he thinks you might think. It is risky for
the patient to think he is homosexual, or know he is
homosexual, so the next move has to be as automatic
and spontaneous as 'Now what in the world makes
you think so?' The statistically most frequent response
will be 'Well, you know damn well I am, doctor.'
There must not be stuttering or obscure retreats into
asking irrelevant questions. There has to be something
done with 'You know I am homosexual.' I say, 'Well,
I don't know what you mean by being homosexual—
it hadn't occurred to me. What makes you think you
are? Do you know anything that points that way?'
And the patient always does. I am trying to put him
on the spot so that he can defend his position. There is
no telling what I will hear. I may hear that he has had
4,572 unquestionably homosexual entanglements with
men. I must still do something, and what? Suppose I
actually did hear about a homosexual experience, then
I would proceed to inquire about the circumstances.
Did he seek it, or was it forced on him, and so forth—
just commonplace inquiries before the final movement. He may say that he finds himself interested in
other people's genitals and wishes they were interested
in his, and feels funny sensations in his mouth and
every time anybody lights a cigarette he has to rush to
the toilet. I must get in now because I want the last
act to work. The last act is when I think I have got
enough, when the person does not seem to be as tense
as he was at the great admission. Then I gaze into the
future and say, 'Oh, yes, I can see how it looks that
way to you *now*.' Then I am through. (p. 114-145)

Note the need for timing the "final movement," the building
up of tension, and then the "last act." For all Sullivan's attention
to anxiety reduction, he lets it build. Again, everything depends

upon dealing with the accumulated anxiety, getting as much anxiety and its associated content out between patient and therapist and changing sharply the patient's perspective of it. "Oh, yes, I can see how it looks that way to you now." (On this occasion emphasis does fall on a temporal consideration.) The doctor understands; the patient is not crazy because he worries about homosexuality. But the emphasis of Sullivan's remark points to other possibilities, the exploration of which is put off to another time. The patient is invited to wonder what those other possibilities are. His own convictions are unsettled. Further, he is not to suppose he knows what is in the doctor's mind. The effect is again counterprojective.

Sullivan has accomplished something more in this exchange that is remarkable for being so unobstrusive. He has managed to have the patient reveal fantasies. feelings and happenings pertinent to the feared homosexuality that under other circumstances would be extraordinarily difficult to secure. It is as if the patient had set out to prove he is homosexual and in proving it, reveals some of his worst fears. "I am trying to put him on the spot so that he can defend his position." What we may not immediately grasp is the position that is being defended. When the doctor approaches the patient like a detective eager to uncover the worst pathology, the patient is driven to defend himself. The position he then defends is of his soundness. But the position Sullivan's patient defends is the position of his sickness! That is because Sullivan has set out not to prove he is sick but to argue that he is well. "Now what in he world makes you think so?" The doctor has positioned himself on the patient's side. Sullivan often sat beside his patients not only the better to hear, but also literally to be on the patient's side; hence one aspect of his fine disregard.[1]

1. See Tinbergen's (1974) Nobel lecture on the value of avoiding early eye contact with children, especially autistic children. Tinbergen's goal is also "the reduction of anxiety and a restarting of proper socialization."

# TWO

# The Other People in the Room

BEING ON OR AT the patient's side helps the therapist to perceive and deal with the "other people" in the room. These "other people" may be obvious, as when a hallucinatory voice shouts at the patient. However,

> the fact is that in a great many relationships of the most commonplace kind—with neighbors, enemies, acquaintances, and even such statistically determined people as the collector and the mailman—variants of such distortions often exist. The characteristics of a person that would be agreed to by a large number of competent observers may not appear to you to be the characteristics of the person toward whom you are making adjustive or maladjustive movements. The real characteristics of the other fellow at that time may be of negligible importance to the interpersonal situation. This we call parataxic distortion. (Sullivan 1954, p. 26)

At any time all our responses reflect mixtures of fantasy and fact. The most commonplace stimulus sets off recollections,

reminders, recognitions that make the present seemingly historical. The method of participant observation is centrally the
method of bringing reality into this history-laden present.

> The great complexity of the psychiatric interview is
> brought about by the interviewee's substituting for the
> psychiatrist a person or persons strikingly different in
> most significant respects from the psychiatrist. The
> interviewee addresses his behavior toward this ficti-
> tious person who is temporarily in the ascendancy
> over the reality of the psychiatrist, and he interprets
> the psychiatrist's remarks and behavior on the basis of
> this same fictitious person. (Sullivan 1954, p. 26)

How is it that we mistake one person for another? How is it
that an appropriate and precise responsiveness to particular
people occurs partially or not at all? We do not expect to confuse a rock with a ribbon but every day we react to Jack as if he
were Jim. In Sullivan's language "interpersonal parataxes" color
social situations to the point where games-playing is more the
rule than the exception. The clearest explanation has been provided by conditioning theory.

People are complicated stimuli and are further complicated by
the many selections the human responder makes as to what
sense data to respond to, (thus the importance of selective inat-
tention). At the same time humans have powerful means to reinforce various behaviors as well as to associate behavior with
anxiety. The great variety of stimuli projected by each person,
the capacity to select stimuli, and above all the habituation or
conditioning to some stimuli allow us to find Jim in just a bit of
Jack, plus John, even Jane. Hence the other people in the room.

Often the "other people" make the patient anxious, just as the
friendly fictions of happier people keep them calm. This anxiety
sets in motion security or defensive operations intended to offset whatever dangers the fictitious persons present. These

"operations," in the language of interpersonal psychiatry, correspond to the resistances of psychoanalysis and the conclusions of existential work. As is true of resistances and conclusions, the security operations both guard the illness and form part of it, like the body's inflammatory response. Determining the pattern of the operations as well as the fictions guarded against (which parallels ego and id analysis) constitutes interpersonal diagnosis.

In short, because the other people in the room (projections, parataxes, or transferences) cause anxiety, the patient develops theories and actions intended to deal with the ficitious persons and the resulting anxiety. Interpersonal technique aims both to determine the projections and to correct them. To do so it acts on the *medium* between people that is filled with such distorting images.[1]

For example, a depressed woman begins describing what a wonderful place the hospital is, its good food, friendly doctors, various bounties seemingly strewn everywhere. We know this cannot refer to the hospital named, but we do not know what theory the patient has about the interview-situation that prompts her to call forth the fiction. Perhaps she is afraid we will punish her unworthy, depressed self for ingratitude. Perhaps she habitually says the opposite of what she means on the supposition that people prefer optimistic statements so that her hate must be changed into love. Perhaps the hospital is a great deal better place than where she had been, and the eulogy succeeds in showing up her husband or sister without revealing that she complains.

All three of these possibilities have a common core: She must suppose we do not want her to complain. She is made anxious

---

1. Implicit in this is the claim that psychosis presents only in caricature what everyday life shows, too. Projections and distortions are not the stuff of psychosis only, but subtly present everywhere. Transference does not only "develop," it is present from the start. It cannot always be effectively interpreted, it must often be acted against. These are the principal differences between the theory of the practice of psychoanalysis and of interpersonal psychiatry.

by the wish to complain and her projection that we do not want her to complain, so that over and over she negates plaintive statements.

Why should she fear our thinking her a complainer? She may have a theory she carries into most situations—that people love the uncomplaining. Perhaps her father actually did, in contrast to what he felt about the patient's possibly plaintive mother. That would certainly be a large nugget to chance upon so early. It is not likely, however, that we could trust the discovery if she happens to find out how pleased we are by it. Nor would her knowledge of the connection necessarily affect her behavior. By discovering her misperception through our eyes, she would likely feel "put down" and would have even more reason to be anxious. We must first diminish her working supposition's hold on the interview, or else "facts" she tells us will be fictions of the uncomplaining kind.

Nor can we reassure her by remarks such as "I love complainers;" she would not believe us if she so much as heard. She might even substitute the word hate for love in keeping with her projections, at which point we would be set back badly. Her supposition is partly unconscious, strongly adhered to, and must be dealt with indirectly.

Counterprojective remarks separate Jack and Jim without calling attention to the confusion. Essentially they make confusing Jack and Jim difficult by Jack's behaving in ways uncharacteristic of Jim. Such remarks include role-playing plus a great deal else that is best called counterrole playing. By distinguishing the therapist sharply from what the patient perceives him to be, these statements lessen the anxiety resulting from the projection, paving the way for the continuing establishment of fact.

Perhaps the clinical situation calls for the doctor to separate himself from a father image. This will not be easy because the role doctors learn is fatherly, and when the doctor acts as if he were a doctor, he triggers the responses that one has learned to make to fathers.[2] In that case the patient is not seeing or responding to us. She is seeing a doctor or a father or both. The facts that we may be older, male, and doctors all make the projection believable. To stay silent before the projection confirms it.[3] If we are conscious of, and want to limit, the extent to which stereotyped roles grip the interaction, we can attempt to clear this medium of its projections by means of counterprojective statements.

The patient's confusion of doctor and father (if indeed that is occurring) provides an option: we can strike at the projection by separating ourselves either from the father or from doctoring. The two attempts at separation will illustrate that almost anything said about a projected figure tends to move the figure out of the medium between the two parties. For example, a socially conventional announcement like "No doubt your father was a man of his word" can accomplish at once an acceptable turning of attention to the father, the creation of an ambiguous atmosphere which the patient can explore, and the psychologically dissonant phenomenon of someone who may be thought of as the father making statements about the father. The patient must for a moment think **with** the therapist about the father, not of the therapist as the father.

Suppose, on the other hand, that the therapist says, "no doubt, your doctor is a man of his word." This is likely to be even more startling than the father statement; doctors do not as a rule say much about themselves, and certainly they seldom raise the issue of their truthfulness, no matter how much patients may be concerned with it. Startling statements, however, occupy a distinct place in this technique. Sullivan was impressed

2. The protest, doctors do not act as if they were doctors, they are doctors, throws this problem into the sharpest light. If we see ourselves as being the job role we have, there is that much less chance of speaking freely enough in the role to be counterprojective. There are, however, those who do not want to leave the doctor-role for a moment, because the doctor loses part of his power when he stops acting like a doctor.

3. We may ourselves believe it, enjoy or exploit it to the extent that it will slip into what I call the social unconscious.

ıly by the extraordinary frequency of projection (as Freud ııad been by the frequency of repression); he also noted a strong human tendency not to hear. Put in the language of today, most of us spend most of the time "in our own heads"; we are a good deal more schizoid than admirers of the human race like to believe. In order to catch people's attention, therefore, startling statements may be necessary.[4]

As a general rule, statements about people who are present and events that are recent startle more than references to absent people and remote events. Sullivan frequently mentioned what elaborate works of fiction emerge from efforts to clarify recent events prematurely—so much for the traditional medical history's first attention to the present illness! "No doubt, doctors are men of their word" would be less provocative than references to the particular doctor.

Such a statement would also bring into sharp relief that stock character, "doctors," as would "fathers" for "your father" and invite comparisons between the actual example, "doctors," and the patient's experience with physicians. This is different from the counterprojective statement about fathers. The therapist is the patient's doctor; he is not her father. It is therefore more realistic, more forgiveable, to confuse the doctor with doctors than to confuse him with fathers. In turn it will be easier to separate "doctors" and her experience with actual doctors from the present physician. The much more important transference confusion of the present doctor with the father will not resolve so easily.

This comparison suggests a paradoxical principle: the more closely the projected-on person resembles the projection, the more easily will the medium be cleared; and in consequence the less thoroughgoing the counterprojective activity need be. This is equivalent to stating that the more realistic the projection, the less unconscious it is, and therefore the more open to detection. However, the principle neglects those instances in which the unconscious meaning and the actual behavior of the projected

4. Furthermore, as Chekhov illustrates so vividly, even startling statements may not be heard, so that the Sullivanian practitioner has a good deal more leeway than some would think.

on person coincide. For example, suppose I act like her father. This is the most precise, and dangerous, significance of counter-transference: when the patient's and the doctor's transferences fit.

In that case our two counterprojective statements are largely equivalent. Insofar as the doctor acts like a father and is reacted to like a father, references to doctor and father have largely the same impact. The decision as to which to mention turns on another consideration. Do we want to attack the projective field through the patient's past experience with her father or through her actual present relationship with the doctor? That it is possible to do either with this technique contradicts those who find it presentbound and unhistorical.

What follows is part of an interview by the author. Note how the real historical past is illuminated as a result of counterprojective statements and that this illumination is purchased at the price of less fantasy material (which associative techniques would secure). The social fantasy system, those other people in the room, is clarified, however. The implication is that these figures were once real: that was how the patient learned about them.

*Postinterview reflections:* PT has been complaining of feeling burdened and in pain. He has resisted seeing the possible link between these feelings and his difficult circumstances, and he has therefore done nothing about those circumstances. Furthermore, PT's complaining is tiresome; TH has no desire either to empathize with him or to confront him. He is delighted to manipulate PT from an expert's distance.

PT: My back aches.
TH: It's no wonder in view of your circumstances. (This attempts to move the complaint out of the medium between PT and TH, into the relationship between the patient and the world, what I have called the screen.)

PT :  My mother asked me to take my sister's bed up to the third floor. (Note that TH will resist any temptation to connect bed, back, sister, mother, etc.; there is to be no search for symbolic connections.)

TH :  She is no unmitigated blessing. (PT is very little attentative to what TH says; so that this complicated thought will probably be responded to on the basis of whatever word in it happens to catch PT's attention. This will be a clue to what PT is thinking that TH is up to.)

PT :  She gave me the car Sunday. (This suggests that PT took TH's last words as being an attack on mother; certainly their tone was not friendly. PT therefore defends moth - er.)

TH :  It's more than you've been getting out of this relationship. (Since TH has been seen as an attacker with whom PT does not, as yet, ally himself, TH decides to separate himself from himself. Such a remark as 'God forbid anyone should criticize mother' would allow TH to remain on the attack and at the same time challenge PT's implied position that mother should not be attacked, but it would run the risk of PT's staying on mother's side and continuing to feel TH is attacking him. TH decided to withdraw to safer ground.)

PT :  The Tofranil made my mouth dry. (Happily this had been prescribed at another clinic, so that PT may be siding a little with TH.)

TH :  Such are the miracles of psychiatry. (TH is not taking any chances! Another possibility would have been one of TH's favorites, "What else is new?" Said with a shrug, this can shake even firmly planted great expectations.)

PT :  My mother isn't sure I need to come. (This may indicate a willingness to talk about mother; it may not. In either case, TH has learned his lesson. Any critical remark he makes about mother will be elaborately balanced. This can be done by pointing up her good qualities or PT's gratitude to her or by saying something bland about her.)

TH: She sure thinks about you a lot. (TH would have liked to say, "Well you may not need to come, but it sounds like she does!" This would require considerably more preparation.)

PT: Once she told me I was the most important person in her life. (This slipped out, right on the heels of "She sure thinks about you a lot." Apparently PT picked up its positive aspect. TH will therefore ride this current of feeling between mother and son, until a clearly opposing one appears.)

TH: You must have loved her, too.

PT: I feel she would do anything for me. She would!

TH: A relationship like that can be very precious. (PT's account of the relationship, no matter what "truth" it contains, suggests a projection onto TH of PT's own doubts or even negative feelings about mother: PT must persuade TH (himself) about mother's goodness. As a result TH is elaborately non-doubting. He wants to remove any need to defend mother that exists in the current clinical situation. Otherwise he will hear only positive things about mother.)

PT: She moves her bed into my room when I'm sick.

TH: She *feels* you need her. (Note how differently this sentence reads if the emphasis falls on another word.)

PT: Once I asked her not to walk with me to school and she looked sort of sad.

TH: There may not be a whole lot else in her life. (Another pro-mother statement. TH is preparing for the "other side": PT's likely resentment of mother's protectiveness.)

PT: She said that my father was very quiet. (This is developing almost too fast. PT may feel it is safe to say these things to TH because he is seen as the positive mother. That can only reinforce PT's dependence, and with it, PT's resentment of dependence. It is time for a move.)

TH: So it all fell on you.

es TH a sharp look.) I felt all stuffy and tight.

ɔ wonder. What *would* she do if you sneezed? (TH
ɩlas removed himself from mother and put her "out
there." PT is to learn how to deal with mother out there.
But there is no obvious way to deal with a person at once
so loving and so smothering. If PT is not to feel foolish in
TH's eyes, this must be acknowledged.) It wasn't possible
to speak out or to keep quiet. (The two conflicting elements have been separated, or widened and balanced.
TH does not want to offer a solution, even if he knew
one. That would be a fresh instance of protectiveness and
again a reinforcing of PT's dependence. Hence: God
knows there might be *something* to do!

While Sullivan sat beside many of his patients, he looked
with them at the social fantasies gradually coming into view out
of the medium between them. He did not play the role of the
blank screen onto whom the patient could project his transference fantasies. The blank screen was to be out there, focused
and explored as the "other people" made their appearances. The
implication of counterprojective statements is, I am Jack, not
Jim; Jim is out there.

# THREE

# Managing Conflict

WE KNOW SULLIVAN developed much of his method working with schizophrenic patients. In Sullivan's formulation these people grow up under hazardous conditions from which they learn to be elaborately circumspect; they cannot afford, for example, the dramatic self-absorption of hysterics. They have to dissociate (some would say repress) both their aggressive and their sexual interests (some would say instincts). These interests stand ready at any time, and particularly if stimulated, to break out of dissociation and disrupt the patient's vigilance and circumspection. Then the divided self of schizophrenia becomes undivided but at the same time confused and disorganized. Therapy with the chronically divided self also threatens to become confused and disorganized if the outer persona and actual inner life are too abruptly confronted. Sooner or later they must be at least partly confronted—if integration is to be achieved—but the when and how of that make up technique. The journeyman electrician in the earlier example was not schizophrenic, but Sullivan's approach to that patient sketches in broad outline how the more complex technical demands of the schizophrenic patient can be met.

Sullivan supported first the patient's need to lie. "Oh yes, and the payment of two percent of one's income to this fund for the sick and wounded is almost never neglected by good union members, I gather." "And one, of course, which you have never violated." The patient felt supported because he did not feel suspected; these are counterprojective statements. Sullivan has offset any tendency the patient had to project onto Sullivan the patient's own suspicions of himself.

Then he supported telling the truth. "Well, of course, you understand that I have no suspicion about you, but your voice sounded odd when you mentioned it, and I couldn't help wondering if it were preying on your mind." This is also a counterprojective statement but one directed at a very different projection. Sullivan has himself brought about this second projection (and the resulting confession) by the process I have called widening and balancing. First he was elaborately unaccusatory. This supported the patient, but it also placed him in a more and more fraudulent position. Sullivan was therefore in danger from a second projection, not now of being thought accusatory but of being thought undermining. The patient must eventually feel: This man is making me lie. Sullivan must now offset this projection. He can do so by becoming the person who wants the patient to tell the truth. He becomes the one who does not want anything "preying" on the patient's mind.

We will understand the need for such complex calculations when we understand the schizophrenic person's experiences of family life. This conflict-engendering or double-binding experience leaves the patient imprisoned.

Sullivan's contentions about schizophrenic family life grew from his reconstructions of his patients' experiences. I have suggested already that his method makes possible a historically true reconstruction as opposed to the rich inner-felt fantasy reconstruction of psychoanalytic method. That his reconstruction was historically true for many of the cases has been demonstrated not only by others using his method but also by others using very different methods.[1] We can therefore anticipate the schizophrenic patient's family experience and, as a consequence,

1. Lewis Hill (1955) is a good example of the first and Adelaide Johnson of the second, by what she called "collaborative psychotherapy" (1969).

what he or she has learned to anticipate from human relationships. Even the crudest advance information of that sort will
help enormously.

Catatonic family experience offers a simple model that will
put the technical problem in focus (Hill, 1955). As a rule catatonic people are very afraid, very nearly frozen in their fear and
therefore cautious, "good," and obedient to heroic lengths.
They have had so much prior experience with parents unable to
tolerate aggressiveness or independence, often literally threatening suicide or madness if such appear, that the patients' public
faces are spectacularly noncommittal. Except for occasional
blind rages, they can be depended upon to bear our most misguided efforts without complaint. Of course now and then a
swear word may pop out or half of an obscene gesture, but no
one is more puzzled and embarrassed than the patient.

The patient presents a noncommittal, uncomplaining front,
behind which smoulder large dissociated interests. The patient
is sent to a doctor because these dissociated interests have
shown themselves in some embarrassing, incomprehensible
way. Perhaps the patient has been swearing quietly at mother.
Sullivan saw his first job as showing the patient that he could
make sense of incomprehensible matters; further, that he could
make this sense in a bearable, even comfortable way. In a field
largely without the anesthetics of other medical specialties, this
ability to operate quickly and relatively painlessly is a prime
mark of the expert.

Suppose the patient hates his mother, but does not know it
(the ideas and feelings are dissociated), or if aware of it cannot
understand why because he has been elaborately educated to
believe in mother's goodness and the importance of respecting
parents. Further, if he does know how he feels and even why he
feels that way, the catatonic person is terrified to show it. He
keeps a poker face.

One more fact and the interpersonal stage is set. Catatonic
persons quietly exude rage and fear, for no dissociative process

is completely successful. People entering the interpersonal field of the catatonic themselves "catch" this rage and fear and become wary in their turn. The result can be a great constriction of therapeutic freedom. Add to this the effects of many of our psychiatric training programs and it becomes difficult to know who is the more catatonic, doctor or patient.

As a result, the catatonic person presents seemingly impossible clinical difficulties. We cannot go along with his "goodness" without sacrificing his dissociated interests, and we cannot share his dissociated interests without offending his goodness or conscience. And to compound the impossible, the patient will almost certainly project onto us both his constricting conscience and his rage. Not only will he feel obliged to keep his sexual and aggressive currents contained, he will believe us angrily bent to the same end: not only intrapsychic conflict of the most apparently irreconcilable kind, but conflict spread out over the surrounding others who become as much the patient's jailer as he is himself. Imprisoned indeed!

How then are therapists to approach psychic elements each of which stands guard against the other?

> . . . a patient may say, 'Well, he's my dearest friend! He hasn't a hostile impulse toward me!' I then assume that this is to explain in some curious fashion that this other person has done him an extreme disservice, such as running away with his wife—or perhaps it was a great service; I have yet to discover, from the interview, which it was. And I say, 'Is that so? It sounds amazing.' Now when I say a thing sounds amazing, the patient feels very much on the spot; he feels that he must prove something, and he tells me more about how wonderful his friend's motivation is. Having heard still more, I am able to say, 'Well, is it possible that you can think of nothing he ever did that was at least unfortunate in its effect?' At this the poor fellow will no doubt remember the elopement of his wife.

And thus we gradually come to discover why it is necessary for him to consider this other person to be such
a perfect friend—quite often a very illuminating field
to explore. God knows, it may be the nearest approach to a good friend this man has ever had, and he
feels exceedingly the need of a friend. (Sullivan, 1954,
pp. 20-21)

The passage begins with an improbability that Sullivan un-
derscores, about the patient's "dearest friend." "It sounds
amazing." Put on the spot, the patient defends his friend. Sullivan is playing on the patient's self-esteem and widening the gap
between assertions and the likely facts. Into the gap Sullivan
puts, "Well is it possible that you can think of nothing he ever
did that was at least unfortunate in its effect?" The friend is sufficiently defended, no one is expected not to have at least some
unfortunate effects, so that it becomes possible to remember
and relate the elopement. However, his friend's alleged perfection lies nearby: the fact and the perfection must stare uneasily
at one another. A conflict has been surfaced and kept open.

A statement is challenged, the patient's self-esteem threatened, his anxiety rises, and with it his defenses. This in turn effects a countermovement back to the friend's behavior because
that too is a dynamic element in the patient's mind; it must
eventually be heard from. Sullivan suggests another, later
countermovement back to the patient's positive feelings for the
friend: perhaps he was his only friend. Essentially the truth
emerges through a series of countermovements that Sullivan
sets in motion.

This dialectic flows back and forth between transitional
statements. Some are very smooth.

When the interviewer wishes to change the subject,
he can make the transition by a more or less adequate,
and at least superficially truthful, statement which
definitely says, in effect, 'Well, now, that brings up
the topic of so-and-so. Eh?' The patient might wear

himself out trying to guess how it brought it up, but
at least the interviewer has taken him by the hand and
led him to the new topic. There are a good many times
when the interviewer may use some little comment
such as, "Oh yes, well, sometimes that's due to so-
and-so. I wonder if by any chance you've had experience of that kind?" In other words, he moves from one
thing to another quite smoothly, so that the other person feels that this is really a very clear, collaborative
inquiry. (1954, p. 47)

Others are accented.

In my case I usually begin to growl, rather like a ball
bearing with some sand in it, just to indicate that
something is about to happen. I want to drop what is
going on, emphatically—not in such a way that it is
forgotten forever, but with such emphasis as to dis-
turb the set, as the old experimental psychologists
might call it. I want that which has been discussed not
to influence that which is now to be discussed. Suppose the person has just been showing me what an
unutterably lovely soul he has. I will then sort of
growl a bit as a preliminary to saying something, like,
'With what sort of person do you find yourself really
hateful?' As a matter of fact, I probably wouldn't do
anything quite that crude. But the point is that as long
as he is full of the idea of convincing me of his beauti-
ful soul, it would really be uncouth for me to proceed
smoothly to attempt to find out how the devil he is a
nuisance. But with the accented change, he may forget
what he was talking about. People are apt to get a
little insecure, you know, what it is suggested that the
weather is going to change, and the predictions aren't
dependable. In any case it causes a little pause, a sort
of empty pause, which is not being smoothly, socially
conversational. And then, without commotion—
without startling the patient  I introduce the new
topic. In this way the later data is not poisoned by the

exploration that was in progress before, as it might be
with a smooth transition. (1954, pp. 47-48)

The patient is being managed, the interview moved along,
and the realities clarified by means of the dialectic that Sullivan
creates between what the patient thinks he, Sullivan, should
hear, and the literal truth. Every effort is made to play down the
conflict between fantasy and reality, which must be anxiety-
provoking. Sullivan hopes the patient will "forget what he was
talking about" in the momentary confusion that the diversive
statement creates, and enter freely, unselfconsciously, into another current of discourse. In this manner, conflicts can gradually surface and be worn away.

> Then there is the abrupt transition, at which, I am
> sorry to say, many interviewers seem to be past mas-
> ters—and I should not wish to encourage them to im-
> prove their art. Nevertheless, it has its uses. I am not,
> however, suggesting a transition so abrupt that the
> patient is suddenly so startled that he can't guess what
> on earth the interviewer has said. I mean, rather, that
> a new topic is introduced which has relevance, but
> which is introduced at what would be described as a
> socially awkward point, and without warning. This
> sort of thing may be done to avoid, or to provoke,
> anxiety. (Sullivan, 1954, p. 48)

"Well, is it possible that you can think of nothing he ever did
that was at least unfortunate in its effects?" "Well, of course you
understand that I have no suspicion about you, but your voice
sounded odd when you mentioned it, and I could not help wondering if it were preying on your mind." These statements usher
out fantasies and usher in facts. Others may carry the patient
through an upsetting period to definitely reassuring material.
"Oh yes, I can see how it looks that way to you now." "Well,
hell, you must have felt terribly sore sometimes in the past."

These take fearful ideas or self-accusations up onto common-place ground and prepare for a fresh examination of the past or future.

Note how seldom questions become part of this technique. Questions, except rhetorical ones, can be dangerous because the answers may lead precipitously to anxiety-laden material. Too much anxiety will result in an abrupt end to truth telling.[2] Moreover, anxiety will lead to defensive behavior, thereby re-inforcing rather than extinguishing the neurosis. Questions are also seldom useful because the patient often does not know or cannot admit the truth. At most he can point to the pain. The interviewer's job is to find the painful truth and help the patient face it.

On the other hand, too little anxiety signals that no danger-ous truths are being approached, that we are being given an accurate account of matters psychopathologically sterile. The key concepts are conflict and keeping conflicts open. Premature resolution of conflict will prevent both the full exposure of con-flicting elements and their being worn away or reshaped in the dialectical process.[3]

One spectrum of transitional statements goes from smooth to abrupt. Another goes from commonplace to innovative. A transitional statement can afford to be innovative if it rides an already strong current in the patient. Commonplace transi-tional statements can ride the conventional.

> The patient I shall discuss had, among the many dis-turbing aspects of a schizophrenic psychosis, decided that he had never been married to the person who claimed to be his wife. But it is safe to say that the

2. This relationship between questions, anxiety, and distortion is painfully evident during the med-ical review of systems. Doctors are trained to ask a great many questions, many of which examine the most painfully private matters. Rapid and intense increases of anxiety are therefore almost everyone's experience of the traditional physical examination and history. It requires all the doctor's authority to keep the patient answering at all. That authority is seldom great enough to prevent distortions.

3. This is comparable to the adversary method in law. Also, recall Sullivan's statement, "There is a difference between being indirect and being obscure."

marriage was most certainly clear to this patient.
Schizophrenics most of the time have access in awareness to such things as the marriage ceremony they
participated in; it's there; it's an experience, and they
can't get rid of it. But the position of this patient was,
'I never married this woman. She is not my wife.'
(Sullivan, 1956, p. 369)

This is the first current, "She is not my wife." How to reverse
the current?

Sullivan guessed that before the patient had reached this flat
denial there may have been a thought "many of us have about
our disastrous performances." "How could I have been fool
enough to do that?" It is what Sullivan calls "an inquiring doubt
business," which like the full-blown obsessional state often
precedes schizophrenia. He therefore does not attack the denial
directly. He hopes to capitalize on the prior experience of
doubting.

"I can understand your having *doubts*, or even a tendency to
deny the marriage." He introduces the idea of doubting, but, he
does not want the patient to take up the doubting possibility at
the moment. The patient will be better able to work on it alone.
Schizophrenic people seldom react to anything new, on the
assumption that what you don't appear to know, won't hurt
you. Sullivan hopes that

> . . . when things are quite calm and there is no per-
> sonal pressure from my presence, there will be a ten-
> dency for the patient to think, 'Why, I did marry that
> woman. Now why do I say she isn't my wife? Oh
> yea, that doctor! He said doubting or denying!
> Christ, yes! I suppose that's the fact. I got so used to
> saying, 'How in hell could I have married this woman'
> that finally I decided I hadn't (1956, p. 370)

The patient's knowledge of his marriage is not repressed. It is
denied. What Sullivan calls a "minimum positive operation"

may succeed in restoring the doubting and replacing the delusion, where direct attempts will only remind the patient of prior unhappy human contacts so disturbed that the "schizophrenic process flowed in." Participant observation deals with the fact that most attempts to correct psychopathological phenomena only make them worse; the interpersonal field then contains material reinforcing the phenomena. It will need to be adjusted for extinction.

The doubting statement rides a likely prior current of the patient's thought. It is also acceptable because it is commonplace. In producing movement away from fixed fantasy systems, commonplace statements are often necessary because the more fixed and extensive the fantasy system, the fewer the transitional opportunities offered; there is little conflicting material to ride. Banalities may be the only resource.

The following illustrates the use of commonplace transitional statements against a very fixed fantasy system in a patient otherwise largely uncommunicative. Sullivan argued that these statements constitute almost the sole technical device over a considerable period.

The patient was schizoid,

> . . . a young married woman who is extremely tense, apprehensive, and inarticulate. Her main difficulty, as she describes it, is that she is an inefficent housekeeper who 'lazes' most of the day away. She looks upon herself as a failure [This is an important element of the fixed fantasy system.] Treatment in the case has bogged down, after several months, and the question raised in the presentation of the problem is, What techniques can be used to get things moving again?
>
> The patient is a product of an extremely traumatic childhood, during which she was deserted by her mother and later abandoned to the care of the maternal grandparents by her father, who was himself unreliable. In the grandparents' home she was treated more

or less as a servant; but as she was very gifted intellec-
tually, she managed to finish college and earn a Ph.D.
in economics. She married a fellow student in the
same field and became a housewife. Her husband is extremely critical of her as a housekeeper, and has frequently told her about romantic entanglements with
other women, always presenting these women to her
as romantic ideals. During the ten years of marriage,
in which two children have been born, the relationship
has steadily worsened, with the husband threatening
divorce and immersing himself in his work, and the
wife leading an increasingly inactive and isolated life.
(1956, pp. 371-372)

The woman's gifts and training stand in sharp contrast to her
attitude and situation. The technical problem is "to get her to
wondering what the hell she has been doing all this time and
why she has never felt entitled to object to any of it."

The very lack of outward signs of suffering indicates
how early she accepted as fit and inevitable that she
should be the slave in her maternal grandparents'
home and that she should in some fashion be kept
from associations with other people, presumably
because she wasn't good enough or trustworthy
enough or just didn't have sense enough. (1956,
pp. 373-374)

In analytic language this patient's behavior is ego-syntonic. It
has not become a symptom, but remains part of her character
or way of life. In existential language, it marks her impover-
ished life-space.

One of the values of the interpersonal method is its power to
work against the ego-syntonic. This method does not run the
risk of the existential attack on character, where a confrontation can result in the therapist's being thrown out rather than

taken in; such confrontations are not a part of participant observation. In addition, the difficulty the resistances offer both
Freudian analysis and Reich's character analysis—that the
analyst may not be able to gain a conscious acceptance of his
interpretations—is not a difficulty of the same degree for interpersonal method. Interpersonal method does not seek consciousness or awareness so much as learning. The patient need
have little insight—indeed insight may cause trouble—so long
as the projections and responses to them are worn away.

Thus, commonplace statements are not meant to produce
flashes of insight. They are meant to nudge or gently shake the
established fantasy system.

> I would sort of hound her with commonplace things,
> not because I care too much about the facts them-
> selves at the moment, but because I want her mind
> to begin to reach a little outside the magic circle of
> insulation in which she has been living all this time.
> Otherwise we are just going to get some fine thinking.
> There must be an outward movement of her interest,
> a beginning of suspicion, 'Well, this really wasn't all
> necessary and inevitable.' (1956, p. 373)

Such a gentle shaking—or any shaking at all—could do little
if female slavishness had nothing in the culture or in the patient
to oppose it. "There wouldn't be anything at all odd about this
woman if she had been born a century earlier in the middle of
New England." As it is, women Ph.D.'s "are not the most common thing in the world," but they exist and are not inevitably
lovers of the loom. Sullivan had therefore not only a strong past
current of the patient's interest to ride but the common sense of
an obvious inquiry.

"Under the circumstances, her feeling of helplessness to get
going in the morning rather encourages me than otherwise."
Why should a Ph.D. in economics be delighted at the prospect
of housework? Her very lassitude signals the continuing

strength of the former, up-to-now dormant interest. The therapist can therefore say to the lazy lady, "no wonder you are bored; home economics it may be, but hardly at the doctoral level!" He thus places himself on the side of both conflicting currents!

She may then feel less guilty, perhaps less sick. She will almost certainly be more conscious of the conflict, because the two currents have touched. Conscious conflict is uncomfortable, however, pushing to premature resolutions which are at the expense of one side or the other. "Double statements" are therefore necessary to hold both interests in the mind, together with some fresh element pointing toward a future synthesis.

"Double statements" are also necessary because encouraging one side of a conflict may precipitate too sharp a response from the other. A patient of mine responded to mention of her loneliness with frightening thoughts of fellatio. Mention of fellatio, in turn, drove her back on the desirability of being alone. It was therefore wise to touch on both at once: "No wonder you want fellatio as long as you're so starved for contact." Moreover, a third current is touched by both statements: "as long as" suggests temporal limitation, a different future, hope.

This dialectical method makes use of other statements for which even the word *commonplace* does not suffice. These statements must seem banal, even mindless. "There are lots of pots and pans and they do keep getting dirty" or "When you've done one load of dishes, you've done them all!" Here are fragments of existential method, intended to keep the feeling of her life before her. The very banality of the statements matches the banality of the patient's existence.

Often in such areas we cannot think of anything to say. Then I suggest recourse to long, meaningless statements which nevertheless contain useable words. Such statements are in the nature of projective tests; they throw out stimuli that accelerate the patient's free development of a theme, as is characteristic of "good conversation."

"There is in this household work so much, so much, duty, repetition, movement and lack of movement; one is close to things, insulated, yet so far away!" That is intended to mean anything and nothing, but some part of it may be useable for the development of whatever aspect of the subject the patient chooses. Systematically ambiguous statements leave the patient free to pick and choose; the patient's choices, in turn, should be revealing.

Finally, Sullivan surfaced conflicts not only within the therapy, but in the patient's world outside it.

> You take a Ph.D. in economics, marry an economist, and as far as I can discover, from then on research in economics has been left exclusively to him. Did that suit him? Was that what he insisted on? Did you just accommodate his feelings that it was awkward to have a wife who knew something about his business, or what? (1956, p. 373)

Now he is not afraid to ask questions because he knows the patient does not have the answers. He wants her to ask these same questions of the husband.

He also asks her what the husband "had in mind in advising her in long, ecstatic letters of his great love for another woman some years back."

> I would try to get her to look at that simply as a piece of research or investigation. 'Now here is a very interesting research problem,' I would say. 'One's husband goes off and becomes enamored of some goddess and writes his wife all about it. Now what was he doing? What did he think he was doing?' She doesn't know, of course, she hadn't had any experience in being anybody's husband. Then I ask her, 'But why not find out?' (1956, pp. 374-375)

The husband strikes Sullivan as someone "who has been getting away with murder because he was fortunate enough to find
one of these incredible women to whom it has never occurred
that there is any fun in life or any give-and-take."

> I think one starts her education in what I call the
> *middle distance*, before college and through early
> marriage, winding up with the great love that came
> into the husband's life and had to be embalmed in let-
> ters to his wife. I do not take an interest in current
> events with her husband, first, because I wouldn't
> know what foolishness she might think I wanted her
> to engage in. You see, I particularly don't want her to
> get the impression that I think she ought to rough
> house him and throw some of the bric-a-brac at him,
> because the poor man might take flight. He might be-
> come completely undone. And I am pretty certain that
> he is insecure enough so that she will find, to her great
> astonishment and permanent gratitude, that she can
> manage with him if she proceeds slowly enough along
> the line I have suggested. (1956, p. 375)

Sullivan wants her "literally to lift her eyes above this tiny
little irregular area in which she lives." He also wants her to
learn that she can develop power to change that area. In keeping with her past research interest, he starts her on a research
project into the husband.

> Now I approach the situation in this way because I
> don't see anything malignant anywhere in it. The
> husband sounds more like an insecure tyrant than
> anything else. Maybe he is also schizoid. He also has
> apparently no better grasp on the principle of fun in
> life than to have an almost classically autistic love
> affair every now and then; I wouldn't be a bit sur-
> prised if some of the women he has been so enamored
> of have known nothing about it. Also, I do not feel
> completely discouraged about his perhaps ultimately
> finding that psychotherapy for himself, though unde-
> sirable, is inescapable. I think that he, too, can lift his

sights a little bit without any serious upheaval of
personality and without this marital group breaking
up. I would hope that together they might even
emerge from this sort of numb dullness that almost
asphyxiates them at times, and get a little bit of pleasure out of life. (1956, p. 376)

Sullivan has carried the management of conflicting currents
out beyond the patient into her relationship with the husband.
He intends to surface, manipulate, and hopefully wear away the
conflicting currents (better now, issues) between husband and
wife by widening the scope and understanding of their own
reality. This is a social psychiatry.

# FOUR

# Two Illustrations

I will now illustrate the principles I have been developing through cases Sullivan himself supervised. These were published in 1947, with an introduction by Sullivan (1947) and no direct mention of his supervisory role. Helen Swick Perry assures me, however, that he was the supervisor. The first case was treated and written up by Sarah S. Tower (1947) and the second by Robert A. Cohen (1947).

Among the number of points Sullivan made in his introduction, three seem critical. Patients in this group, he wrote, have been "denied much developmental opportunity" and the "handicap resulting from this must be remedied, at least initially, by *active* participation by the physician." Second, "reassurance is an intricate process depending chiefly on the patient's inferences from superficially unrelated remarks of the physician functioning as an expert in interpersonal relations." Finally, "success in therapy and research is basically dependent on the physician's skill in handling the movements of anxiety in the patient." (1947, p. 125)

Sarah Tower's report details "the measures taken to avoid paranoid development in intensive treatment of an obsessionally defended person with a history of frank paranoid psychosis of brief duration." This report, like the one to follow, is as candid in its account of what did not work to this end as it is helpful in describing what did. I suspect that the change from one to the other was the result of Sullivan's supervision.

> [The paranoid psychosis of brief duration] developed during the winter and early spring of 1942-43, when the patient was twenty-seven years old. At that time he was working under pressure from an overbearing and neurotically anxious department head. And he found himself engaged to be married to a girl in a city at some distance. In midwinter the patient consulted a psychoanalyst, because of increased tension and indecisiveness, and began treatment three times weekly. The indecisiveness applied to his full range of daily occupations, especially to those which involved meeting and talking with people, but applied most intensively to the problem of whether or not to marry. Was this the "perfect marriage"? By early spring the condition had flowered into a paranoid state with flamboyant delusions. He believed, for instance that his office was a cell, that the people who walked up and down the corridor were guards or jailors; he heard others accusing him of homosexuality; and he had a vision, possibly a hallucination concerned with a cart like a tumbrel which was going to take him off to the State Hospital. (Tower, p. 138)

"In March of 1943 the psychoanalyst summoned the patient's parents and discussed with both of the parents the condition of the patient at that time. Hospitalization was arranged and the patient entered a mental hospital in March 1943." He remained there just short of one year; and was referred to Dr. Tower in September of 1944. He had already resumed his work in industrial research.

> When D. B. presented himself for treatment, his chief complaint was 'I feel the pull of people.' As he illustrated this pull with banal incidents such as an invitation to dinner, a suggestion that he join the YMCA to

play handball, a sailing expedition on which the skip-
per 'ordered everyone around,' the paranoid coloring
of the complaint became unmistakable. The complaint
has persisted to the present time, but the coloring has
varied from paranoid exaggeration and justification,
through acute resentment with anxiety, to querulous
defensiveness of a no longer tenable position, and
finally to an habitual mode of speaking in which he
refers to the tension he feels in interpersonal relationships. (p. 138)

The patient was not only tense in interpersonal situations, he
was "extraordinarily uncommunicative." He had to force his
words out, choking, swallowing, wringing his hands, jerking
his head and body, almost catatonically. Dr. Tower "interpreted" this obstructive behavior together with the hostile feeling conveyed, but this had "little ameliorating effect, as is the
case with all verbalized understanding on his part."

In fact he grew worse over the first two and one half months
of treatment. "His feelings of being 'pushed' by women, includ-
ing myself, and 'pulled' by men increased sharply in intensity."
Reversion to a frank paranoid state seemed imminent. "I was
much concerned to counter this trend, but my efforts to make
the patient aware of its fantastic quality only seemed to under-
write the movement" (p. 139). Then, I suspect, came the supervision.

In reviewing my handling of the case, an outstanding
feature seemed to be the way in which increasingly
I had coddled this patient, partly in an almost automatic—even physical—endeavor to facilitate his
labored communication, partly from my original fear
of the paranoid possibilities and increasing concern
over them. I realized that the tone of voice especially
had come as it were to woo his confidences, even
though the content of my comments remained fairly
objective. Clearly this was playing into his fantasy
of being 'pulled.' (p. 139)

She was supporting not opposing his projections because the way in which she spoke undercut what she said. She then set about to counter this role. Again, the change was a change as much, or more, of tone and attitude as of content.

> Accordingly, an abrupt reversal of this attitude—accomplished largely by realization of what I was doing but evidenced again by change of voice, this time from concern to flat matter of factness—was followed by a 'forgotten' appointment, a unique occurrence with this obsessional patient; this was rapidly followed by more down-to-earth talk of perfection, ending in painful disclosure of the patient's feelings that his mother is vulgar. (p. 139)

Now there was a change in the *patient's* content. He began to talk, and to talk critically, of a parent. Dr. Tower does not explain how this came about, although it is a commonplace of counterprojective method. Earlier I suggested what may be the explanation: counterprojective activity moves the projections out of the medium and onto the shared screen, away from the relationship and into the discussion; therapist and patient then can examine the projected figures. In this case they found a "vulgar mother." Insofar as the projected figures leave the medium and are "seen," the patient feels less influenced by them. To the same extent he is less in the grip of his paranoid fantasies, because the fantasies are the reflection of what he is feeling in the relationship. In psychoanalytic language, this patient's "transference psychosis" was being "resolved," but not by interpretations, instead by what resembles a relearning or extinction process.

> For the five months following, until a three month summer intermission, the work continued with—for this man—increasing productivity and spontaneity and with a steady broadening of the basis of the

relationship between us. Throughout this period and
to the end of the second year of treatment, I repeatedly and baldly stressed the professional nature and
limitations of our relationship in an endeavor to
counter his flamboyant fantasies of intimacy with me
sufficiently so that the real intimacy of the physician-
patient relationship might develop. Moreover, having
seen the deflationary effect of a sharp, unsympathetic
tone of voice on a paranoid process, under the pressure of my own disinclination to become involved in
a paranoid twosome, I found that this verbal statement of non-intimacy was automatically backed up
and made real in tone of voice in proportion to the
paranoid coloring at any particular time. In sharp
contrast, I tried to meet any offerings of simple real
feeling, either friendly or hostile, with warmth and extreme simplicity and with a minimum of interpretation. (p. 139)

Again the interpretation was minimal. The assumption was:
this patient does not need so much to learn about life as to learn
to live. Once the patient accused Tower of hanging a picture of
mountains at the foot of her couch "to influence me in the direction of greater strength and masculinity." She responded
sharply, "You think I would go about dealing with you that indirectly, by hanging a picture on the wall?"

In this instance, my unreceptive stand—while it
prevented exploration of the fantasy as such and kept
me as a somewhat real figure out of the paranoid in-
volvement—also led to the patient's turning sheep-
ishly to consider: 'It seems I'm just beginning to learn
what it is to be direct with people, you and others, in
the last few weeks.' (p. 140)

Note that her intervention "you think . . ." is barely a question, at most a rhetorical question. She rendered her directness

as much by the manner of speaking as she did by its content; she became a direct person. And the patient's supposition, that people deal with him indirectly, was in this case made fully conscious. She must have felt that the idea was already very close to full awareness; indeed it had been discussed already. Her frank reference to it then became a rebuff to wallowing—"Why are you still doing that?"—perhaps on the assumption that his parents had encouraged or exemplified wallowing.

She closed the case report with a reference to two other patients successfully managed in the same way.

As Tower remarked, her active "rejection of a transference relationship, the refusal to exploit it, appears to be contrary to the basic principle of psychoanalytic technique" (p. 140). Certainly, at these points, I did not analyze the patient's highly pathological mental and emotional processes. The procedures described belong to a process which must precede analysis in persons with as weak a grasp on reality as the patient—and to a greater extent with frank psychotics." This process she described as the "education" of the patient to a real physician-patient relationship. This educational process, she added, "may need little specific attention" with neurotics "or run concurrently with transference analysis."

She did not write more as to what this educational process consisted of, particularly as to how this learning differs from analytic learning, or how it might run concurrently with a transference analysis that was, she had remarked, quite contrary to it. She had, however, taken a position widely adhered to—that Sullivan's techniques were useful perhaps exclusively in the presence of psychotic phenomena and as part of the preparation for psychoanalysis. Participant observation was seen as a "parameter" of analysis.

We will return to these issues later, when a better groundwork has been laid for their discussion. Most of all we will need to grasp the therapeutic processes in psychoanalysis and participant observation, their similarities and principal differences.

Robert Cohen's remarkable account of the second patient opens with a brief description of her several hospitalizations, then a vivid portrait of the patient as she first appeared to him, leading quickly to the first extended material—her family history. Typically, emphasis falls not on fantasies but on family facts.

> The patient is the youngest of three daughters of a retired educator who resumed teaching to pay for his daughter's treatment. The father is an extremely reserved, phlegmatic person with no capacity to express his emotions. Apparently, he tried to give his daughters some emotional support, but when he found himself unable to understand them, he withdrew entirely. During my only interview with him, he was extraordinarily ill-at-ease; he had absolutely no knowledge of his daughter's feelings and fearfully retreated from even the most superficial discussion of them. He was very close to and dependent upon his own mother until her death when he was fifty years old, a fact which may account for his marital difficulties. The patient's mother, in her sixties, is a self-centered, dominating person who has always been demanding and punctilious in the observance of social forms, but quite without interest in people as persons. Her own sister describes her as one who never faces facts, who puts up a false front, and who tries to make out that things are not what they seem. The parents have always been unhappy in their marriage, there have been frequent open quarrels in front of the children, and in recent years they have virtually separated. (Cohen, p. 144)

Note the father has been interviewed, perhaps the mother, and an aunt. Also interviewed was the second sister, six years older than the patient, who arranged for the patient's transfer to the present hospital, Chestnut Lodge, and who spoke bitterly of the parents, broke away from them, and tried to persuade the patient to break away, too.

> This family setting was not one calculated to pro-
> vide any notable degree of emotional security for the
> patient. At the time of her birth, after some twelve
> years of marriage, the parents had given up hope of
> mutual happiness and had begun to drift their separate
> ways, their sole remaining bond being the recrimina-
> tions cast chiefly by the mother. The mother appar-
> ently never had much interest in the patient. It was
> common knowledge in the family that she had wanted
> a son, if she had to have children at all, and the patient
> recalls that at the age of six, she asked her mother if
> she would have preferred a boy and was told, 'Well,
> it would have been nice.' The father did afford her
> some support; she dimly recalls that he sang and read
> to her, that she enjoyed hearing him play the violin,
> and that he would take her sleighing on the steep hill
> in front of their home. But these moments of closeness
> grew infrequent, and except for the events during a
> trip to Europe when she was ten years old, she grew
> progressively more lonely. She was separated from the
> rest of the family by physical as well as emotional
> space. The parents' bedroom and the rooms of the two
> elder daughters were on the second floor of the home,
> while the patient's room along with that of the maid
> was on the third floor. She recalls being excluded from
> her sisters' rooms, and once she broke a window in
> protest against this. But for the most part, she accepted
> her assigned status, played by herself in her room, and
> of course came to resent intrusion on her privacy by
> the others. (pp. 144-145)

She completed a private grammar and then high school education. Except for a year or two she was unhappy, not suc- cessful in her school work, and discouraged from attempting college. She may have grown still more withdrawn during a time of heavy family discord. There were at least two periods of suicidal preoccupation, at eight and nine or ten years later.

After a trip to Europe with her mother, she did begin college work, eventually at a sister's college, and with a moderate degree of social success. This last stands out in the case report. On several occasions she was strikingly popular, even made relationships that persisted at least until the time of the report; yet *withdrawn* and *isolated* are the words used most often to describe her.

> As graduation approached, she found herself sorely troubled as to the future. She wished to go to Chicago and secure a job, but felt too insecure to face the prospect of reaching for an acceptable opportunity. She did not wish to return home but felt that she could not ask her father to support her away from home. A possible solution appeared in the offing when her brother-in-law died and her mother went West planning to remain with her eldest daughter for an indefinite period. The patient then decided she would go back to Cleveland, stay with her father, and try to get started on some type of career. But her mother returned in three weeks, complaining bitterly about the sister, and then there commenced an unhappy period at home with the parents bickering, quarreling, or giving each other the silent treatment. (p. 146)

She moved to a rooming house, held several jobs, attended secretarial school but found it boring. Then she tried teaching in a nursery school, but this too was unsatisfying. Then,

> three years after graduation, the patient managed to transfer from her lonely rented room to one in a college dormitory, and shortly thereafter secured a position as teaching aide in a public educational institution. These two events made a marked differ-in her life. Her social opportunities increased, and for the first time since college she made one close girl friend

and several good ones. Although she took the place of
a girl who had been an outstanding success on the job,
she pitched into the work, mastered it, and displayed
considerable ingenuity and originality in her class
presentations. Nor were her efforts bent only to teaching; despite initial opposition, she proposed and carried through several time-saving and logical changes
which conflicted with established routines. (pp. 146-
147)

Then, so typically, came the unrequited love affair. She met a
graduate student two years younger than herself. He was "diffi-
dent, prim, and somewhat effeminate;" further, he responded
to her affectionate gestures awkwardly and even hostilely.
Nevertheless she felt herself in love with him and when he
turned to someone younger and seemingly more vivacious, she
became deeply depressed, "refused to speak to him when he
telephoned, and was quite inconsolable."

In addition she was forced to leave the dormitory, lost sleep,
appetite, and weight, and finally her job. She went to stay with
her father, improved a little, but fell back again during a visit
with the oldest sister. On her own initiative she sought medical
help and was for the first time hospitalized. Notes from this
hospitalization suggest a paranoid process, and on admission to
another hospital three months later she was clearly delusional
and hallucinating. "In a note to her father at this time she wrote
that, if he wished to know more about her, he should read the
front page of the *Chicago Tribune.*"

From the outset of the patient's treatment with Dr. Cohen,
she "showed no inclination whatever to describe her difficulties." His efforts to reason with her largely failed. Most of all
any reference to her "indecisions" or "dissatisfactions," indeed
any reference to the problematic past, angered her. "She said
that the past was over and done with, that she had liked her
work very well, that she was feeling better and there was no

point in going over old business. She pointed out that it was not her fault that things had gone wrong."

Indeed she was improving socially: She became more friendly on the ward, spent less time on her bed, and dressed neatly. She also kept her appointments with the therapist.

> She then cautiously began to mention that there had been a difficulty aside from her work. In a most careful and tentative way, she related a few details of her unhappy love affair. Several sentences concerning it would be followed by an hour in which she resolutely kept the discussion on neutral topics. Slowly she developed the story of her meeting with Bill, of falling in love with him despite his shortcomings, and of her despair when he turned to another. She had been unable to throw off her feeling of utter discouragement over her inadequacy. Then she began to be tortured by distressing thoughts. First came the idea that she was rejected because Bill was indeed a homosexual. But he had rejected her for another girl. Then came the horrifying thought that it was she who was abnormal and that was why he had rejected her. She recalled that she had felt stronger than he, and therefore she must be 'more masculine.' She recollected that she had turned to her women friends for solace. She recalled that once she had telephoned her best girl friend from her sister's home, had chatted with her gaily for half an hour, frequently laughing over the conversational interchange. When she hung up, the sister had looked disapproving and grumbled something about 'such adolescent behavior.' (p. 149)

She felt her sister had been talking about her and must regard her as immature, sexually and otherwise. "So she must be a homosexual, and with this thought the bottom had fallen out of her world."

After several hours during which no material was produced and every effort to extend the inquiry into other
areas of her life history had failed, I became somewhat anxious and attempted to give her fairly direct
reassurance regarding her concern over her supposed
'homosexuality.' As she began to retreat and to deny
again the need and potential usefulness of treatment,
I responded, among other ways, by advancing the
usual trite arguments concerning the need for self-
understanding—the fact that much could be learned
from one's mistakes—and I made some statement to
the effect that it was important to study what she herself might have contributed to the break-up of the relationship with Bill. (p. 149)

On the ward she once more retreated to her room, com-
plained of headaches, and "while speaking to the nurse, she
broke into a denunciation of the hospital and of the treatment
she had received."

Then she herself broke the impasse with the following note:

These things were made clear before I came to Chestnut Lodge:

1. Anybody in my place would have cracked up.
2. I did everything any girl would have done.
3. Bill was to blame.
4. Being analyzed has no place in sewing me up.
    a. Therefore, if a load is too much for anyone,
       why does their cracking-up indicate any misun-
       derstanding of themselves?
    b. How could I have felt so well at the first hospi-
       tal if there were still things to be explained?
    c. It was a situation in a million, but you seem to
       assume that it could happen again. That's as-
       suming I'm to blame.
    d. It does not make any sense to say anyone would
       have cracked, and then imply that it was my
       fault.

e. Why, now that I am here, does the picture
change, refuting everything I've been told?
(p. 150)

Between the delivery of this note and the next appointment,
Dr. Cohen reviewed the situation with his supervisor. He does
not comment extensively on the patient's note, which is surely
as plain an invitation to an existential encounter as has ever
been written. Nor does he explain how "these things" were
made clear to the patient before she came to Chestnut Lodge.
He did acknowledge to the patient that not only had he not
made himself clear, he had increased her feeling of helplessness.
"In ways of which I was too bemused to be aware (I) had tried
to force admission that therapy was necessary by attacking her
pitifully low self-esteem in the implication that Bill had good
reasons for rejecting her." In other words, the therapist had reinforced her perception of the situation. "My personal contribution to the set-back had been demonstrated to me so vividly
(presumably by Sullivan) that I felt deep concern over the de-
structive operation I had carried out."

The result was, an existential meeting (Havens, 1974), in that
both patient and therapist shared despair. Hitherto, the therapist asserted, he "accepted at face value" her assertions of lack
of interest in psychotherapy, (no, he had not accepted them; he
had argued with them), blinding himself to the feelings of despair. Now he both accepted her despair and acknowledged his
own failure.

I told her that I had received her note and was dis-
tressed over the feelings implied in her questions. I had
reviewed our recent hours and recognized that not
only had I failed to make my meaning clear, but also
that certain of my remarks must have increased her
feelings of hopelessness. I am sure that the exact words
I used were of relatively little importance. (p. 150)

The honesty, the feelings are what matter most in an existential encounter. "Exact words" are the concern of psychoanalytic
interpretation and participant observation.

"She responded that she knew she had a tendency to put the worst interpretation on everything."[1] He, in turn, "thanked her for calling attention to my inconsistencies" (presumably in the note) and "for giving me the opportunity to clarify my position." (Note how he falls back into the language of insight therapy. He actually has not clarified his position; he has abandoned it and shared his failure with the patient. But the treatment is still being thought of as analytic.) Furthermore, he "expressed the hope that she would again let me know if the difficulties inherent in making one's thoughts clear to another should lead me to commit other unwitting mistakes. I did not stay for the entire hour. She had ostensibly remained in bed because she was too exhausted to come to the office." It may be, too, that his not staying the entire hour reflected discomfort in this unfamiliar, existential posture. Certainly it is a far cry from either psychoanalytic or interpersonal expertise.

Again she improved. "She began to go into Washington with the recreational therapist and was pleasantly surprised at her lack of fatigue. She played tennis and soon regained much of her old skill. She started to read, at first newspapers and magazines, later turning to books." "An aunt who visited her found her no different from her old self in any respect, except that she was ten pounds under her usual weight" (p. 151). Nevertheless, "all this indicated a gradual social recovery rather than progress in fundamental understanding of her behavior patterns. At times she regarded herself as actually homosexual."

> At other times she recognized in this thought another expression of a lifelong self-depreciatory attitude, but all efforts to develop some insight into the dynamics of her reactions failed, since they met the stone wall of her inability to discuss her early life experiences and her attitudes toward her parents, sisters, and other significant figures. (p. 151)

1. Compare Minkowski's response (Havens, 1972).

Then "a second episode occurred in which the resolution of anxiety led to a resumption of therapeutic progress."

The patient's father initiated and completed arrangements for a visit. The visit "did not last more than an hour, and part of this time he spent with the administrative therapist and with me."[2]

> The few minutes he spent with the patient produced dramatic results. She came to our hour the next day, but in a more disturbed state than I had ever seen her. She continued to come to the hours, but for the next two weeks she spent most of her remaining time alone in her room with the shades drawn, lying on her bed, eating but little, and speaking only when it was absolutely necessary to do so. The change in her appearance was striking; she looked frayed, dilapidated, and frightened. She described her feelings in superlatives— superlatives of terror and despair. She felt that all was lost. She thought her head was split open, that her brains were filled with blood, and that she would suffer the agonies of the damned and then die. (p. 151)

"I finally got a statement that the distress had begun when her father had told her that the administrative assistant had informed him that she might be able to leave the hospital in a few months or a few weeks. She then burst into a tirade against the administrator, pointing out that her contact with him had been casual, that she regarded him as thoroughly incompetent." This event, she felt, was "just another repetition of the same old persecution—they always waited until she felt better and then beat

2. The so-called administrative-therapeutic split is in large part an outgrowth of Sullivan's influence. By removing therapists from administrative responsibilities it is hoped they will be less likely to have projected on them images of restricting or denying parents. The danger is that therapists may figure such projections are not therefore active and neglect the opportunity to deal with them.

her down—and that the whole affair had been deliberately planned to torture her" (p. 152).

Dr. Cohen tried to deal with her anxieties rationally and to look for hidden sources of them; "her intense anxiety was partially assuaged and she resumed her social activities." But a striking improvement followed on something else.

> Subsequently she was able to recall one other remark her father had made, although she insisted that it was quite insignificant. He had hitched his chair alongside her and said, 'If you can tell me what you have been through, I guess I can take it.' When indirect and direct questions brought no further information as to her reaction to his remark, I described for her an incident from my pampered military career. From my office in a resort hotel in a Rocky Mountain valley, I could look out over our 750-foot, all-weather swimming pool, could see the western end of our private golf course, the tennis courts, the stables where we kept our riding horses, and the ski tow rising to the top of the nearest peak—and then I could swing around in my leather swivel chair and look at some perspiring, trembling bastard just off the boat from Guadalcanal and wonder why in the hell he was irritable and did not enjoy the place as I did. I could say, 'If you can tell me what you've been through, I guess I can take it,' and then go out to the officer's mess for my steak dinner and pie a la mode. (p. 152)

"Most of what improvement the patient has made dates from this hour." She was then able to reveal some of the rage she felt towards her parents and sisters. "She described her life-long feelings of isolation and inadequacy." She gave most of the family history recounted earlier. From that point to the time of the report there were no important setbacks.

What had Cohen done?

This was not a transference interpretation, no matter how much it affected the transference. The patient had been talking about the father, not the therapist; ostensibly she had not been confusing the father with the therapist. Nor did his anecdote further an awareness that she had been transferring from the father to the therapist. On the contrary the anecdote implied father and the therapist might have been alike!

Nor was the anecdote existential. Although he shared his own experience with the patient, it was not an experience like the patient's; he had not been the soldier off the boat from Guadalcanal; he had been the officer who behaved like her father. And, again, there was the implication he had behaved toward the patient like the officer and like her father before.

By the anecdote Cohen separated himself both from his own past behavior and from the father's. The image of that behavior left the silent medium between therapist and patient and was put where the two could examine it. Cohen's statement was superbly counterprojective.

How had the counterprojective statement made possible the revelation of "the rage she felt towards her parents and sisters," the account of her "life-long feelings of isolation and inadequacy," and the reconstruction of the family past already presented? A full answer equals the account of this method's therapeutic rationale to be given in a later chapter. Suffice it to state here that Cohen believed these results did flow from the counterprojective statement and that that statement, by separating him from the father, made it possible to talk about the parents precisely because at least one parent was no longer "in the room."

Later in the treatment they approached her fear of homosexuality. "When she was about six, (a maid) induced her to play doctor; this evidently involved sexual stimulation of the maid. That patient, who had not been spoiled by caressing on the part of her parents, found that she enjoyed the sensation of bodily contact, but this aroused intense anxiety. She looked upon her behavior as indubitable evidence of depravity" (p. 155).

During the early period of her overt illness, "she undressed women in her mind." "To the extent that it had been possible to separate the feeling from the associated horror and revulsion, it seems to be accompanied by a feeling best described as one of aching tenderness" (p. 156).

By the time of the case report, she and Dr. Cohen had not reached her feelings about the mother. Nor was there any material linking that feeling of "aching tenderness" to the mother. We can therefore only speculate as to what would occur in her relationship with Dr. Cohen when and if that relationship, the "aching tenderness" and the figure of her mother converged. My expectation would be that at such a moment Dr. Cohen would once again have to separate himself sharply from the parental figure.

# FIVE

# An Interview

THE FOLLOWING INTERVIEW was done as part of the evaluative process in a hospital clinic. The twenty-nine year old patient came for treatment because she had lost her ability to write. Her personal relationships had seldom been rewarding, but she had consistently been able to work well, especially to write. Now she was unable to write even in her own journal.

PT: And I'd say, this is stupid, Anne, nobody's going to read this except you, I mean, you don't have to be a perfectionist here, at all. Relax. And I couldn't do it. (She experiences an inner quarrel between being and not being a perfectionist. We can guess there is a perfectionistic introject, which, as is true of introjects, will be readily projected on the therapist. TH, however, chooses to postpone dealing with this likelihood, and instead makes an existential statement, a hypothetical translation of what her inner experience may be like.)

TH: As though somebody else was reading it all the time. (Use of the phrase "somebody else" does prepare a little for the likely projection, according to the general rule that talking about an introject reduces projection.)

PT: Always. That's really a good way of putting it 'cause I always feel like somebody was looking over my shoulder or eavesdropping on my mind.

TH: It's probably not hard to get to that way. (This, instead of "who was it?" The latter remark may remind her of an argumentative busybody, someone actually looking over her shoulder and eavesdropping. Any psychiatrist is already too close to this image to risk behaving like it, unless of course he wants to reinforce the projection.)

PT: Well, what do you mean? There were several people. (TH may not have spoken clearly. In any case his statement was not clear. This was in part because he did not want to pin her down, but instead to give her a sentence like a projective test, to draw out whatever was uppermost.)

TH: Several people? (This was probably unnecessary; it also runs the risk of seeming critical or inquisitive.)

PT: It was my advisor who I really respect a lot and is very, very good. She's brilliant, and an excellent writer. I felt like I could not sit down to write anything without her being there correcting my punctuation, my thoughts.

TH: Because she was such a big cheese in all this. (This is intended to be counterprojective, that is, to reduce the likelihood of PT's seeing TH as another big cheese. The implication is meant to be: I don't like big cheeses either, and I am not one.)

PT: Yeah. She's very good. I've always thought I was a perfectionist; I'd never met anybody that was (laughter) such a perfectionist.

TH: This is really not good news, to put it mildly. (Again, "I don't like perfectionists"—I am not one. Also, "it is really not funny," despite her laughter, to offset any manic denial of her pain.)

PT: Right. I felt whatever I did for her was wrong. But then it extended into other kinds of writing.

TH: You mentioned the journal. (In retrospect, this also seems unnecessary, more a reflection of TH's curiosity than of any desire to clear the interpersonal field.)

PT: Yeah, reading the journal, it didn't even sound like me. I'd read them a day or two later and say, who wrote that?

TH: They weren't only looking over your shoulder; they were guiding your pen! (A more existential remark would have been, "They were changing, artificializing you." The actual statement deals with what *they* did, not how she felt. Again, the goal was to separate TH from such dangerous figures.)

PT: I hated them, I didn't like what I wrote at all. It just seemed artificial, not only bad writing but not my writing. (Her hate is probably still more directed at what she wrote, in keeping with her perfectionism, than at the dangerous figures. She is still very much identified with them. TH must therefore go slowly in his attacks on them, or else he will be attacking her.)

TH: The teacher, even for all her good qualities, was probably a little filtering or censoring. (Will she draw back or attack the teacher more vigorously?)

PT: Well, yeah, she is just extremely critical and a fine eye for detail and I don't know, she very rarely praises you for anything and when she does, well I feel really good. (She does not draw back; however, she indicates plainly her need to be loved by these perfectionistic figures. It may therefore be that if TH praises the patient he will reinforce the perfectionism on the theory "I'll get more praise if I'm perfect." In that case PT will probably end up paralyzed and hating TH.

TH: But she's probably not so easy to tell to get lost either. (This is a "double statement." It supports any desire the patient has to tell off the teacher at the same time it recognizes her fear of doing so. It therefore serves as a transition point to the development of either of these themes, without forcing the conflict between them too soon into consciousness.)

PT: Oh I can't, no. My degree hinges on her approval of my thesis. I'm in no position to tell her to get lost (Her fear is first expressed, but . . .) . I did at one point, I had been completely unable to, I had been spending a lot of time with her but I was completely unable to develop any kind of personal rapport, it was always strictly professional relations. I know I was having problems writing this and I didn't know how to tell her about it. I also know I wasn't doing my best work, not only couldn't I think of anything—it would be like my mind closed. So I sat down and I wrote her a letter, it was five pages, single spaced, and I tried to tell her that this was just . . . to me, nothing like this had ever happened to me with schoolwork before.

TH: With schoolwork. (The repetition of a word or phrase is a commonly used associative device in psychoanalysis to develop fantasy themes. Note here how it impedes the development of the factual narrative so characteristic of interpersonal work.)

PT: No . . . like I said before, there are lots of areas where I didn't have any confidence in myself, but schoolwork I had always had confidence in myself.

TH: More so than in these other areas. (Again, an underlining, so characteristic of associative method. It is not pursued enough here to do more than interrupt the participant observation.)

PT: Yeah, well, I guess I'm trying to say that I think schoolwork and personal relationships, I could always do work. Anyways I tried to tell her this and after she got the letter she was very nice, she said, I found your letter very touching, and I told her about, and I told her I didn't mean it to be touching necessarily, I was just trying, I was saying it more as a matter of fact, it was a description of the condition.

TH: She found it touching. (This was said with emphasis—derisively. TH is eager not to be confused with the teacher. His interest might be experienced as the teacher's pity was.)

PT:   Meant to evoke your sympathy.

TH:   She found it kind of moving or touching. (Again heavy-handed. There is to be no mistake TH's difference from the teacher.)

PT:   Yeah. Look, in a way, I was glad that she responded at all (laughter). (TH has succeeded beyond his hopes. He has drawn out the "do not pity me" theme so far that the opposing current surfaces: "All I'll get is pity, I'd better be content with that!").

TH:   Thank God for little favors. I mean, what more could a poor student expect? (Perhaps too sarcastic. TH is now a little overcome with his own success and cleverness. Nevertheless . . .)

PT:   Yeah, exactly. This is what keeps occurring to me. It didn't at the time, but subsequently it has. (Is she trying to please TH, who's so obviously pleased with himself? She'll be the perfect patient and gain TH's love. "What keeps occurring to me" may have just occurred to her for the first time, but by backdating it enough she'll confirm TH's cleverness. One difficulty with a manipulative method like participant observation is that the patient may outmanipulate the therapist.) I've gotten to the point where . . . my schoolwork I'm grateful for any little crumb I get.

TH:   Any little crumb that is thrown to you from the great teacher. Yeah, well, God forbid you should be a patient under those circumstances. (He must prepare for her clinical gratitudes! Otherwise she will be thankful for the little favors collected in the clinic, then resentful, with reinforcement of the neurotic pattern. There must be no favors from the clinic.)

PT:   Well, frankly, I'm a little suspicious about that.

TH:   After that experience I wouldn't be surprised. So the great lady was at least willing to be touched by it. This communication. (PT has indicated a suspiciousness about treatment. TH does not want to deal with this yet.

An interpretation of her transferring old attitudes to the treatment will probably result in what Sullivan called "a fine piece of thinking" on PT's and TH's parts and little else. What would be worse, such connecting remarks by TH may make her more suspicious: "I must watch out, this man discovers all sorts of arcane connections." Perhaps, however, TH could have tried, "God knows the treatment may be no better." As it is, he goes back to the teacher.)

PT: This was towards the end of January, going on February, and I thought something's got to give, and nothing ever did. I mean by spring I'd finally managed to get a twenty page outline written which normally I would have written in ten days. And it took me two to three months. And it is lousy.

TH: You were down and out. (Another bit of existential method, dangerous here because PT may see it as a crumb of pity.)

PT: So then after spring vacation I came back actually to do the research on this thing and as long as I was doing the research in the library I was fine, but as soon as it became time, about the end of January to begin writing it up, I just blanked again and I couldn't write anything and, all the physical things started returning, I mean I started throwing up and my heart. . . .

TH: Your heart?

PT: Racing, racing, racing all the time and my stomach, and that was what first got me going to the counseling center last fall 'cause one day I almost fainted and I thought, this is just stupid.

TH: . . . you needed a doctor.

PT: Something got to stop, but another thing too. I keep wondering why I'm doing this, a couple weeks ago I sat down to write one morning and I didn't feel particularly nervous or anything but I did . . . all at once, I'd no sooner sat down than my stomach started going bluh bluh and I'd keep gasping for breath all the time and um, so I went away from the typewriter to sit down and read and before my eyes and I could feel my heart and then it sort of occurred to me that anybody else would have said to hell with this thing a long time ago.

TH: But not you. (TH aims to support the part of her wanting to quit. Again, it puts TH over against the demanding teacher and, as we shall see, demanding parents.)

PT: But why am I? (Has TH invited this inquiry by his earlier "you needed a doctor?" Doctors are often expected to know the answers. In which case TH will have fostered some great expectations difficult to fulfill.)

TH: There's this teacher.

PT: There was the teacher, the pressure from home. There was the fact that I had completed ten years. . . . (Here is the first clear bridge to home. Note TH has not inquired about home or even underlined any associative material that might lead there. In my experience the reasonably consistent application of counterprojective techniques by itself leads to the earliest introjects, as if in drawing more recent figures out of the medium and onto the conversational screen, the way is cleared for the earliest figures.)

TH: Would you say also that you're content with little favors? It doesn't take much to keep you feeling. . . . (Compare this with TH's earlier "I mean what more could a poor student expect?" This was a sarcastic comment, but the sarcasm was directed against a behavior of the patient's from which she had at least temporarily been enabled to distance herself. And she responded agreeably and developed the theme further. The earlier comment is also a question but a plainly rhetorical one. In contrast, the present question is not rhetorical. It asks for an acceptance of insight into an unfavorable aspect of PT's personality, and, to make matters worse, is followed by a still more demeaning comment. Naturally, PT does not respond agreeably).

PT:  I didn't used to be.

TH:  . . . Touching.

PT:  I didn't used to be at all.

TH:  So content with little favors. (Perhaps TH has repaired his blunder by his last two, essentially existential comments. That is, having distanced himself by the insight—seeking inquiry, he has re-established a better relationship by being where the patient is.)

PT:  But I have become that way. I used to be content with little favors in personal relationships but never as far as school went.

TH:  But in personal relationships you'd take little favors. (Again, no more than a repetition or translation of PT's statement. TH will be cautious for a while.)

PT:  Yeah, I'd take all kinds of crap from people that I should not have.

TH:  Sometimes you get used to that. (This is what I have called elsewhere a hypothetical statement or extension (Havens, 1974), and is part of existential method. The implication is "sometimes *one* gets used to that," i.e. TH joins PT in another experience PT may have had, one closely connected to being "content with little favors." In this context the existential remark may also be counter-projective. TH places himself with PT and apart from those who dish out the crap.)

PT:  Uh huh, yup. What would happen is I would just keep my mouth shut and all of a sudden I would explode. I'd get very angry. That's the pattern. (Note how much of clarifying and interpretive work PT is doing for herself.)

TH:  You said it applies only to your work now but your relationship with your teacher and personal relationships, but I suppose it goes back to you know who. (Again note the avoidance of questions and the use of a blank spot at the statement's end, for the patient to fill in. If TH is right, that is if the contemporary figures have been cleared, then the old ones should pop up immediately.)

PT: My parents. Oh definitely. (No apparent resistance)

TH: You don't have to be in a fancy clinic building to hear that line. (TH is taking no chances. He wants to reduce as much as possible any tendency the patient has to understand the family transfer matter *psychiatrically*. Such a tendency to isolate or intellectualize the understanding would reduce its emotional power for change in the therapy. As a result TH wants to separate himself from psychiatry and the clinic as much as possible. Otherwise PT's understanding may be restricted to the clinic or to her work with her psychiatrist.)

PT: Of course, it goes back to my parents. I mean I thought I had. . . . (Note *she* is arguing for the reality of the transfer effect, not TH.)

TH: That would be a little . . . really (TH backs away from all this insight. He certainly does not want to support or applaud it if only because, as we shall soon see, the insight has not worked.)

PT: I thought I had gotten that situation straight, the relationship with my parents, a couple of years ago when I moved from Seattle. And for the most part I did. It was only since this year, the first two years I was here, I worked and supported myself while I was going to school and didn't take any money from my parents at all and we seemed to get along okay under those terms, my parents have money, and they would always say to me do you need help and I just didn't take any money from them, I didn't want their money because they used it like a weapon. They had done that several, several times, in the past where if you do something such and such, you're not getting any more money from us to go to school. They did this when I was an undergraduate.

TH: So again you have to be thankful for somebody's favors. (TH had not been listening. PT had just told him of a time when the parents had withdrawn their favors. TH is still very pleased with his insight and perseverates.)

PT: Uh huh. So anyway I had been working for over a year ("Anyway" is a common transitional term used by patients. Here the transition is somewhere between accented and abrupt: a polite brushoff.)

TH: I didn't mean that it wasn't inevitable there would be someone to be thankful to. (Neither very graceful or accurate. TH isn't aware of his lapse.)

PT: Yeah but (a transitional phrase now fully abrupt!) it's not so much a matter of gratitude as it is what they withhold that I would. (She gives TH a second chance.)

TH: What they don't present you with. (He takes it.)

PT: Yeah, which is, I think, approval.

TH: Approval? (Does TH really need clarification of this?)

PT: Well, they're very confusing because on the one hand they've always said, go ahead and do whatever makes you happiest, dear, but then, as soon as I do something they don't like they certainly register their displeasure.

TH: Now then it's got to be . . . of the time. (A combination of ambiguous request for projections plus a temporal extension, that is an attempt to share extending the experience over a longer period of time, e.g., "it's been that way a long time.")

PT: It's everything, for the most part, not so much with my father, my father just never says, he rarely says anything unless he's quite upset.

TH: Maybe that helps you get used to the clinic work, anyway. (An abrupt and crude counterprojection; actually TH may have been saying too much.)

PT: What do you mean, I don't understand the connection. Whereas my mother is—very much a perfectionist and she had a very good job before she got married and since getting married, she had me, they were married in July and I was born the following June which they hadn't counted on at all because my dad was still in school, so she had to give up her job. And on account of me she's never worked. And now, she just has four kids at home who are 15 and 12 and a house that is much too big for them. And she still keeps saying she has all this house-work, oh my God she has all this housework and she's afraid to go out to work and anyway she's made the house the center of her life and she's very much a perfec-tionist you can eat off her floors. And I was always a slob by comparison, so it began with little things like that.

TH:  Why is it more fun to eat off the floor, than off someone's table? (TH does need to separate himself from her parent's values, for she has said a great deal and may become afraid TH will be found on the parents' side. Nevertheless this rhetorical question is complicated and perhaps not rhetorical enough. Note in what follows that it produces a repetition of something PT said earlier. PT feels TH may not understand and must have things explained again.)

PT:  I don't know. It's like I said, sometimes it's very confus-ing to me because it seems well first of all I feel that no matter what I do it somehow will never be quite good enough for them. The other thing is, on the one hand they say, you know, do what makes you happy dear, or what I began to tell you about was, I had been working here for a year and a half and then the people I was working for were moving to Washington and I had the option of either moving to Washington or staying here and finishing my degree. So I decided to stay and finish my degree and it had been really hard for me going to school and working as much as I did. So what I thought was, I'm going to borrow money from my parents for several months, get this thesis written and done and then

get a full-time job. Instead of spending a whole year
going to school and working part-time. I wanted to get a
full-time job. So I talked to my father about it and he said
fine, there was no problem, they would lend me the
money. And they did. Now all I keep getting is why
aren't you through with this thesis? What's taking you so
long? We keep giving you money and money and not
from my father, just from my mother. And at Easter I
tried to tell her about the problems I was having and she
said, I couldn't believe it, she said, for Christ's sakes,
dear, what are you letting that intimidate you for? No
degree is worth this. Get out. I . . . the fucking degree just
cause they wanted me to!

TH:   What else is new? You were thankful for little favors
anytime. (This seems abrupt but it works out well. PT
continues to develop the theme, more particularly to
present fresh information. TH had in mind the danger of
her coming to feel TH would think her ungrateful, as no
doubt the parents did, at least the mother. Such a fear on
the patient's part would stop the narrative flow. TH
therefore emphasizes her inappropriate thankfulness lest
she feel he feels she should be thankful.)

PT:   Then she went on to talk about the new sofa she was getting in the living room or something.

TH:   . . . but then of course you were thankful for little favors.

PT:   I was just so angry with her because I was trying to tell
her something that was important. (TH does not mention the similar experience with her teacher because that
might be interpreted by PT as an attempt to take her attention away from the parents in order to protect them.)

TH:   Who listens? (TH had not been listening himself earlier. It
is important to acknowledge that. This will not favor his
identification with the parents because he is willing to
acknowledge the failing. It may also strike against any
narcissistic expectation on PT's part that everyone should
listen and understand.)

PT: And she wouldn't listen.

TH: Who listens? (Notice that this seemingly discordant remark does not interrupt her flow.)

PT: I wanted to drop out of that degree program around two years ago after my first year because I didn't think it was what I wanted, it wasn't really relevant to my interest and unfortunately, I had to go home for something and I got this whole spiel, about my gosh you've invested a year and put money into this thing you might as well stay and get the degree. You can't get a job without a degree. And I thought well, all right.

TH: And now she's asking why you're still in it. (To encourage any long narrative flow the listener must speak for and about characters mentioned in the flow. Otherwise the speaker will stop, embarrassed at talking so much because of wondering why the other person is silent or what he or she is thinking. Remarks such as the present one also keep the projected figures out of the medium and on the narrative screen in front of patient and therapist.)

PT: And now she's saying, well for crying out loud, dear, if it's going to get you that upset, don't you have enough sense to get out of there.

TH: What did you say to her? (This question is not designed to elicit information. It is intended to put some distance between the patient and herself, that is, to get her thinking what she might have said that she didn't. As I have repeatedly emphasized, participant observation is like training or learning. PT is to learn new responses, new ways of dealing with mother. Put differently, she is to abandon her old projection of herself, too!)

You could say it's touching to listen to me for a little bit, that's enough for me. Well, that certainly is one advantage to coming to the clinic anyway. That certainly strikes home. (TH is getting ready to end the interview and he must prepare PT for its inevitably meager results.)

PT:   What, coming to the clinic because people will listen?

TH:   Yeah, people will listen if you tell them something touch-
      ing maybe. (In psychoanalytic terms all this is directed
      against a premature and unworkable transference. The
      danger is very great, because therapists do listen and
      often commiserate, thereby directly reinforcing the par-
      ent-teacher projection. No wonder transferences are so
      often unworkable. The medium undercuts the message,
      i.e., the therapist's behavior undercuts his interpreta-
      tions.)

PT:   Well, I don't care about touching anyone, actually.

TH:   You were hoping there would be someone at the clinic
      touched by your story. (TH directly contradicts her! He
      does this because he *wants* her to disagree with him, not
      to be the one who is satisfied with making others feel
      sorry for her. This is comparable to what Rank called in-
      creasing the will to resist. Of course TH is also separating
      himself from anything in her clinic experience that might
      reproduce and therefore reinforce her earlier experiences.
      For that reason he becomes elaborately sarcastic about
      the clinic.) Lord knows there's bound to be somebody
      around that would be touched by an unhappy story.
      They might not do anything about it or understand but
      they might be touched by it.

PT:   That's my concern. (Not meaning "it's my business, not
      yours," but "this is what I'm worried about.")

TH:   Who the hell is going to do something about this, because
      you know, you're sort of down to your last dollar at this
      point, right? Your personal relationships are lousy and
      your work is lousy and even your writing to yourself in
      your journal is lousy, so more or less, what the hell is
      there worth living about. . . . Right? So you come to the
      clinic and hope that someone will be touched by your
      story. (TH is trying to respond in a way sharply different
      from the way her teacher responded. The purpose of this

is not to give her a "corrective emotional experience" in Alexander's sense. The purpose is to distance himself enough from the previous figures so that he will not elicit the response they did. TH does not have much faith in corrective experiences that take place once or twice a week. He wants a more powerful relearning tool than that.)

PT: I just need to get rid of (note the word "just." Actually what she's referring to is no minor matter. But she is still putting herself forward modestly, even waifishly. No wonder people pity her. TH, however, is going to take her problems more seriously than she does. This will involve some existential extending, but its purpose is not to be and stay with her, but to clear away the projections. Of course this will encourage fresh projections and these will have to be dealt with in their turn.)

TH: Maybe you'll be lucky and find someone who'll be more than just touched by this story, because it's been going on a long time and you're not a spring chicken anymore.

PT: No. I'm twenty-nine.

TH: Twenty-nine. You're moving along. (Note the almost caricatured turning away from reassurance. Again, this is to distance TH from the teacher and probably the parents.)

PT: I certainly am. That's one of the things this year that has been sort of becoming certainly something that I'm more sensitive to, than I ever was before.

TH: Twenty-nine isn't sixteen anymore. (Does TH seem insensitive? No doubt he will to some. In fact, PT does not mean she's sensitive to being 29 but to being 29 and getting nowhere. Plainly, TH is very sensitive to that. It is a matter of the pieties vs. the practicalities.)

PT: No it isn't. And I sort of look at what I've done and feel like I've done very little with my life, other people have. . . .

TH: You don't want another quarter century like the last one. Might as well be in the grave. I get the message. (TH is probably overdoing his statement of concern. He is inviting PT to expect more of psychiatric efforts than they are likely to produce.)

PT: If I really believed that, and if I had any courage, I would put myself in the grave right now, spare myself the time and the trouble. (Almost inadvertently TH has made an evaluation of her suicidal potential. This has been done without having to ask about suicide, an inquiry that so often touches off at least a little guilt in the patient.)

TH: You wouldn't be the first, you wouldn't be the first. (Here is an example of a counterprojective management of a suicidal threat. TH is implying: if you're considering suicide in order to threaten or hurt me, you haven't got a chance. With this patient he is also saying: "I am not touched." Contrast TH's remark in an existential approach: "Maybe it isn't possible to bear these feelings.")

PT: Bothering people for another twenty-nine years.

TH: Yup, you were hoping somebody would be touched. Well, maybe you'll find somebody at the clinic who will do a little more than that.

PT: I have to somehow change, I have to change my opinion of myself and the way I live and the problem is I think....

TH: But you're still at the typewriter. (At first glance this appears to be an attempt to firm up the insight about perfectionistic introjects, as something to leave with her from the interview. However, this is not TH's purpose. Indeed such an insight might be more depressing than useful. What TH wants to do is to get as full an account as possible of PT's actual situation. By the somewhat cryptic typewriter comment he hopes to stop her list of forbidding personal objectives (e.g. "change my opinion of myself" etc. etc.) and find out what else is going on. It might have been better to say: What else are you up against?

Such a direct comment, however, might be experienced as too abrupt a turnoff; in contrast, cryptic comments often produce a little retrograde amnesia, which would be useful here. In any case TH soon does manage to extend his knowledge of the facts, at which point he is quietly hopeful. He will have put himself in an enviable position in the light of what can be accomplished by such one-shot interviewing efforts: PT will have revealed a considerable number of her difficulties and diminished any expectations she carries that the listener has been rendered hopeless or discouraged with her.)

PT:  In the same pattern.

TH:  Or another clinic, and another doctor, right?

PT:  Yeah.

TH:  What the hell *is* different? (Another rhetorical question. The implication is: nothing's different. At the same time this is an ambiguous transitional statement. It invites PT to think of something that is different. Note that she picks something that is different in the sense of worse.)

PT:  Exactly. Exactly, except that, I don't know, I get really scared when I think about different things and I get really depressed when I think about things staying the same. (Perfectly in tune with the transitional statement. First she says "exactly" on one side of the transition, then she goes over to the "different things.")

TH:  Right, so you're really caught between the sad things and the scary. Around and around they go. (Very existential and again inviting the conclusion: TH pities me.)

PT:  Like I've often thought that I dragged this whole thesis thing out this year 'cause I'm afraid of that, I don't know what I'm going to do when I'm through with the thesis. Well, then what's going to happen? And . . .

TH:  Then you've got to make a real tough decision. (Again very existential. TH has probably become worried about PT as a result of being introduced to these "different things" that are still worse. He may therefore want to move closer to her.)

PT: Well, I'm going to have to decide whether to stay here or whether to move somewhere else.

TH: Yeah, and then there'll be various suggestions made, I imagine. ("Not by me.")

PT: Oh, probably. Well you could just, the thing is I have a boyfriend here who wants to get married, he's going to school and he'll be here, he finished his course work and he'll do his pre- and stuff next year. He'll be probably stuck in Washington for the next couple of years and I hate Washington and prefer not to stay here at all and that's just one factor.

TH: Another . . . getting married, you may have seen enough of marriage to have your doubts about that. (TH has suspected, without much evidence, that PT's family is big on marriage and solidarity while not being a good advertisement for either, and he wants to get aw¬y from that.)

PT: Oh, definitely. I've never wanted to get married. Well, all my life I've said I never wanted to get married or have children because of my parents' marriage and because I took care of kids, my youngest, I mean my oldest all my life and I just, housework and kids; you can throw them out the window.

TH: And yet this guy wants to get married. (Again counter-projective. Note that the slip is ignored.)

PT: Yeah, then of course my parents don't like him because he's going to be an academic and will never have any money. (TH is having trouble finding a neutral place to land.)

TH: Well it seems like a dark picture to put it mildly between your mother and your father and your teacher and your boyfriend and God knows who else. Not knowing what to do, now we're at the clinic. Well maybe you'll find somebody who's more than just touched by the whole thing. Well I appreciate your coming. . . . (Just a "touch" of reassurance; TH was afraid more would encourage unreal, perfectionistic expectations and less would seem cold and indifferent.)

PT:  Oh, thank you.
TH:  I think they'll be making an appointment for you.
PT:  Who do I see now?
TH:  Let's find out.

# SIX

# The Interpersonal Perspective and Techniques

Each of the great schools places its investigators and therapists at a particular angle, we can say, to the patients. This is a
concrete position: in psychoanalysis behind, in existential work
close to, in Sullivanism beside the patients. But the angle or
position bespeaks a psychological perspective that is not so easily described.

The attitude of inquiry is characteristic of objective-descriptive examining; questioning and testing are its expressions. In
contrast, psychoanalysts often deny that they take a position;
their goal is neutrality and an evenly hovering attention;
silence and occasional emphases express this effort toward neutrality. In still further contrast, existential therapists seek not
neutrality but its opposite, the patient's position; these therapists mean to be where the patient is. The tools are empathy,
the phenomenological reduction, translating and extending, together with a willingness to encounter the patient and to
change. (Havens, 1972, 1974)

Participant observation, in turn, requires that we sense what
others are doing to and with us and that we be free to act in that
social field. Just as existential method asks that we give up our
position for that of the patient, so participant observation asks
that we give up our position for whatever position the needs of
counterprojection dictate. This requires alertness and flexibility,

which in turn demand apartness. One must not be "taken in." [1]

The medical attitude of inquiry is pointed at the patient. The objective-descriptive examiner means to find something wrong with the object-patient and to do so by asking, looking, touching, testing. And the patient is enlisted as an active informer-collaborator of the doctor; he is to question and observe himself. The theory behind this method is also plain: there is conceivably something "wrong" with the patient, and this something yields clues—signs and symptoms—spontaneously or in response to the questions and tests of the examiner. Further, the theory is that these signs are method-stable: they are steadily enough present not to flee at our approach. The patient may want desperately to conceal his tumor; he may not be able to recall the symptoms, but this uncooperativeness will not alter the physical signs.

We know that this method has produced remarkable results in the nonpsychic area. It remains a principal tool of clinical medicine, however much fortified by still more objective ,instruments. On the other hand, the objective-descriptive assumption of disease states and its method of active uncovering encounter obstacles in the psychic realm that have thrown the whole effort into dispute. The use of the patient as a voluntary reporter was, as indicated, an obvious weak point. It was largely given up by psychoanalysis as soon as the extent of unconscious phenomena became evident. Some means that did not require the patient's active cooperation had to be invented, par-

1. That is, give way to the "numbing feeling of reality." To caricature the principal methods, objective-descriptive examiners are like detectives, closing in on the diseases. Psychoanalysts can be compared to sensitive detecting and recording instruments that also compute connections among the almost infinite number of bits of free associative material. And the existential therapist! Here is the nursemaid, the priest, but perhaps more nearly the lover, who will be with and share himself with, quarrel and make up with his beloved. Finally the participant observer resembles an actor or an imposter, acutely attuned to what each person is doing to the other and free enough of inhibitions or perhaps identity to act the required parts.

ticularly because active cooperation interfered with the release of unconscious content and, indeed, could be used to substitute for it. The result was a method of passive cooperation that has required an equivalent passivity on the part of the doctor. [2]

The resulting passive, waiting attitude of both analyst and analysand struck against the so-called resistances. These had to be analyzed in turn, but with little agreement that the neutral, interpretive techniques would suffice.[3] Further, psychoanalysis yielded enormous amounts of verbal material that were readily taken up into explanatory reconstructions; the reconstructions were often more impressive than the extent of improvement of the patients. There was the occasional possibility that the patients were meeting the theoretical expectations of the often authoritative analysts; then indeed the work was "writing on water." In the case of all these difficulties the psychic material would not submit itself satisfactorily to the objective operations of the medically trained therapists. The result was a great need for fresh methods and perspectives.

The two principal new approaches each took as its point of departure a different weakness of the established theories. The existentialists questioned that trustworthy knowledge of another could spring from any method separating therapist and patient. The so-called objective understanding of science objectified the patient, it was argued; the patient became a type or example of something already known. The person's uniqueness and his unpredictable place in a historically unfolding process made impossible any fixed, schematic knowledge of a person. Only through a full acceptance of the other, only by seeing the

2. For a more detailed account of the objective-descriptive and psychoanalytic attitudes, see Havens (1973). The reader should be warned that no account of the psychoanalytic attitude will secure much agreement today because psychoanalysts have taken on many aspects of existential and interpersonal developments, sometimes unwittingly.

3. See, for example, the numerous discussions of this point in the recent volume *Confrontation in Psychotherapy* (ed. Adler, Myerson, 1973).

world and himself from the other's point of view could a valid basis of understanding and treatment be established.[4]

The interpersonal attitude, in contrast, saw the weakness of the established positions not in their objectivity but in their pervasive subjectivity.[5] Although objective-descriptive and psychoanalytic method had striven mightily for objectivity, the effort had been frequently rebuffed and was nowhere fully successful. Sullivan, like Meyer, was a keen critic of both psychoanalysis and Kraepelin (Sullivan, 1946). The latter had attempted to attach a specific psychopathological picture to each etiological agent in psychiatry, a project quickly discredited.[6] And the diagnostic system he established, although still dominant three quarters of a century later in its major distinctions, remains under steady attack. For its part psychoanalysis had discovered that the mere presence of the analyst attracted the very neurotic process analysis was meant to destroy: hence the transference and transference neurosis. Freud turned this into an advantage of the method: the neurosis could now be dealt with at first-hand. But there remained at least two difficulties. Perhaps the transference occurred much earlier and more pervasively than the first analysts had perceived; this certainly seemed the case with at least some of the patients, and the formulations of the ego psychologists suggested it was true in part of all the patients. Moreover, what assurance was there that the relatively neutral, rational, verbal, interpretive, insight-centered method of psychoanalysis could control the neurosis now rampant at the very heart of the treatment?

The existentialists believed that something beyond either

4. The chief exponents of this point of view in the United States have been Carl Rogers and Rollo May. The chief European figures have been Binswanger and Minkowski. The Americans are more practical and optimistic than the philosophical Europeans.

I like to ask whether such an approach as existentialism, that questions every schema of understanding, does not secure its popularity only in times lacking an agreed-upon body of theory.

5. One feels already in this remark the link between interpersonalism and behaviorism.

6. The work of Wernicke's student Bonhoeffer (1910) was especially devastating.

subjectivity or objectivity could be achieved by narrowing the distance between subject and object. The interpersonalists, in their turn, transformed the meaning of both therapeutic objectivity and neurotic subjectivity. A true therapeutic objectivity, they argued, required frequent activity on the therapist's part if the incessant neurotic subjectivity were not to engulf the clinical situation. The social field was dominated by projections and roles attributed to others and played out. These roles might themselves be neurotic; their interaction perhaps invariably was. Therapists need not await the neurosis; they were already victims of it.

Put in other words, the ego of interpersonal theory is not a rational executive presiding lucidly over the relations between id, superego, and the world. The ego is so heavily infiltrated by social experiences that no one can speak of an autonomous ego and mean autonomous from society. The ego has learned roles; in addition, it is at least partly composed of introjects, parts and wholes of significant others, who therefore continue to stand between the patient and reality. One result is that transference becomes parataxis: the distorting process is present and ubiquitous from the start.

It was as if the fish had at last discovered its medium, the water. Here was a challenge to objectivity, this warcry of a social relativism, that threatened not only the treatment postures of both objective-descriptive psychiatry and psychoanalysis but also the stability of the data of the first and the autonomy of the ego of the second. At his most grandiose Sullivan is supposed to have announced that no one was schizophrenic when they talked to him. All the gossip about his own mental state, even the claim his patients were not truly schizophrenic, failed to shake the observation that some patients when subjected to his method, did seem less schizophrenic; the stability of the old symptoms and symptom clusters was being undercut. Moreover, psychoanalysis, while moving toward more and more therapeutic dependence on alliance with a supposedly neutral ego or ego components, saw that ego described as far from autonomous at all. Perhaps the therapist had only allied himself with a subservient child-self deeply in fear of authority. In any case, how could one know?

I act as if I were a doctor. Oh, yes, I "really" am, but to what extent, when and, in what way? And the patient! Is he now a patient? He says he is, but does he mean it? The clinic and the world become possible fictions.

One essence of the interpersonal attitude is this suspension of belief before any presentation of the self. Of course it holds in mind that shrewd, small question, "What is he or she up to?" Of more significance, however, we are asked to explore the world fictively, as if the world were an imaginative creation. And we are to clarify the world at the same moment we may be one of its richest fictions!

## THE TECHNIQUES

Still another way of differentiating the perspectives of the different schools is to specify the data each illuminates. Objective-descriptive work seeks symptoms and signs, psycho-analysis fantasies, existential work feelings, and interpersonal psychiatry the facts. Of course these data of the methods are not exclusive: facts may lead to fantasies and the reverse; sharing the patients' felt world, as in existential psychiatry, often leads to the discovery of the facts of that world as well as fantasies about it. Nor can one method ever be used to the total exclusion of others. Yet we approach the particular perspective of each school in these data of first interest.

Of course not only data are of interest but also the particular defenses utilized against revealing data. Here again each school method cuts in a different direction. Too clear a separation would be misleading, but psychoanalysis does work wonders against repression, being and staying set themselves especially, I think, against denial, while participant observation both manages projective tendencies and allows their factual basis to emerge. I will try to summarize in a more schematic way than I have done how this last is accomplished.

We can divide the interpersonal techniques in two, those that displace and those that reduce projection. The first are those I have called counterprojective: directed against the "other people" in the room. The purpose of these interventions is to move the projections out of the medium between therapist and patient onto the space or screen before them: these are displacing remarks. The goal is not to reduce or eliminate projections but to move them.[7]

Displacing remarks have the inner structure: That introject you are projecting on me has one or more, often negative, features. Because the patient generally does not know he or she harbors the introject or is projecting it, however, no open reference is made to the processes of introjection and projection. Such a reference may or may not come later. Instead the overt form of displacing remarks is simply, "so-and-so (the person who has been introjected) has this or that feature." In essence, displacing remarks speak about the "other people" in the room.

Speaking about introjects displaces the projection of them away from the speaker for the same reason that pointing toward or asking about clay figures of mother and father during play therapy directs the projective tendency away from the therapist and toward the clay figures;[8] projection follows attention. We do not need to use concrete embodiments in the treatment of adults because, with many of them anyway, their abstract capacities allow words to stand for things. In short, when I talk about someone, the remarks puts that person out there before us.

Furthermore, it is often wise to speak negatively about the introject. Doing this may give permission to the patient to do

7. I am particularly indebted to Dr. Michael Madow for this distinction.
8. I owe this comparison to Dr. Michael Charney.

likewise. It also serves dramatically to separate therapist and introject in circumstances where the therapists' typical professional behavior too closely resembles the actual behavior of the introjects. Perhaps father was detached, careful, neutral-seeming, uninvolved—some therapists will have to behave in unaccustomed ways to do more than confirm that projection.

Of course speaking negatively of parents terrifies many schizophrenic people. Ambiguous or double remarks may then be necessary, for example, "well, mother probably wasn't an unmitigated blessing."

On the other hand, the more openly paranoid someone is, the more directly hostile the therapists will need to be toward the persecuting figures. Those who still believe that "taking the patients' side" in this way fixes or reinforces paranoid ideas should try the counterprojective method and learn that the opposite of fixing or reinforcing occurs. The reason it does not, I believe, is as follows: people project feelings because they cannot take responsibility for them; they must be shared. (That is in part because one source of the hostile feelings is the introjects which indeed originally were outside.) When therapists express what the patients feel toward the hostile introjects (or now, pro-jects), therapists are helping the patients to bear what they cannot bear alone, that is, what they have to share. To the extent that therapists "take over" the feelings, the patients can give them up. They don't want them anyway; that's why they project them in the first place.

Many therapists will reply, patients should take responsibility for their feelings, or less moralistically, one goal of treatment is patients' acceptance of their feelings as their own. This amounts to saying, projection is pathological and when therapists permit or even welcome it, surely projection is being encouraged.

In fact, the interpersonalists are as set against projection as anyone, perhaps more so in that they claim to detect more of it than anyone else. The only issue is the issue of method. Here the interpersonalists make a specific claim. Until the patient is able to bear alone the unacceptable feelings or ideas, no attempt to force the patient to bear them is likely to succeed. On the other hand, sharing the feelings and, above all, acknowledging any reality at their root opens the way to their acceptance and then disavowal or reduction.

The remaining techniques are counterprojective to just this end. At the same moment they seek to validate the patient's projections, they seek to undermine them. This seeming paradox lies at the heart of the method.

A common form of interpersonal utterance begins "No wonder you feel. . . ." This is a double statement in that the realistic basis of the patient's feelings is acknowledged at the same moment something else is implied: there may be other ways to feel. Note that the appeal is to experience, not to the content of spontaneous thought, as in analysis. The steps are, acknowledgement of experiences, to feelings that are therefore understandable, to the possibility of different feelings. These steps, so quickly listed, may take years, when the depth of defenses is great and the feelings difficult to acknowledge.

## CONTRAST WITH PSYCHOANALYSIS

The claim that there is a realistic basis for projection is still disputed and serves to separate many psychoanalysts from interpersonalists. It is widely acknowledged that paranoid delusions, to take the extreme instance, contain a germ of truth. It is not always acknowledged, despite the work of Niederland (1960) and Johnson (1969), that paranoid delusions are often disguised reproductions of actual events.

Put differently, projection is still understood by many as a defensive transformation along the original lines Freud formulated from the Schreber case: unacceptable impulses may be transformed and projected. When Neiderland discovered in his historical investigation that Schreber's father had in all likelihood actually done to Schreber what the latter imagined was being done to him in his psychosis, a fresh explanation of projection was made possible. This explanation became still more convincing when Johnson, through her collaborative psychotherapy, demonstrated that at least the initial schizophrenic hallucination and delusion reproduced actual events from the patients' lives in faithful detail. Indeed the hallucination, like a literary metaphor, told more of the real truth of the events than literal statements would.[9]

The new view of projection was in a larger context not new at all. It restored to psychiatry one of Freud's original suppositions: that many symptoms were memories. The same supposition was always implicit in Sullivan's thought because for him psychiatric phenomena were learned, that is, they not only arose out of interactions with others but were quite literally handed down in the form of behavior. The related psychoanalytic concept is identification, in the case of paranoid delusions, identification with the aggressor; thus introjection and projection. An instinctive process may be necessary for introjection; social experience certainly is.

We are not forbidden from espousing both views, when the evidence favors an instinctive mechanism at this moment or a behaviorist one at the next. What we are forbidden from doing is utilizing the psychoanalytic method or the interpersonal method alone to resolve the dispute. Psychoanalytic method makes possible the maximal fantasy and transference development. Interpersonal method does the reverse. The clinician who wants to sort out fantasy from fact will therefore need both.

Many psychoanalysts have argued that transference interpretation together with the therapeutic alliance keep analysis oriented to reality. In the therapeutic alliance the realistic ego of analyst and analysand sort out fantasy and reality; this is called reality testing. Why then is interpersonal method, in particular counterprojective work, necessary?

9. For other evidence in support of this contention, see Silberer (in Rappaport, 1951).

When therapists appeal to the realistic egos of their patients they have no way of being sure that any response is directed by the facts and not by the relationship. The patient may look honest, sound honest or even be honest, but the honesty may spring from an honest desire to please the therapist, not the truth. The result is what Sullivan called, "wonderful works of clinical fiction." Then the realistic ego has proved to be a dependent and obedient child, which therapy has reinforced. On the other hand, insofar as counterprojective statements succeed, they obviate the need to please. There is no value in lying to someone who, ideally, cannot be seen as either hurting or rewarding one. By assuming and counteracting fictions, by a thorough-going fictive attitude, interpersonalists avoid being taken in.

## EGO WORK

The second set of techniques can be summarized as ego work. This is not work with the ego, in the sense of a therapeutic alliance. The work is on the ego which stands against or distorts personal development. This ego is the executor of social experience which, in Sullivan's words, has "distorted the person to less than he might have been."

In this respect Sullivan took more seriously than many analysts the battle an early Freudian formulation postulated between impulse and society. A later formulation saw the battle as between life and death instincts with the ego mediating as best it could the strife. Sullivan remained faithful to the earlier formulation that put less weight on instinct and reason and more on society and compromise.

In the conflict between distorting society and restless impulses, interpersonal therapists proceed as experts working out the most serviceable compromise. Old habits must be changed, new ones learned, impulses gratified but not to the extent and at the time desired. The mediator is now the therapist's ego, a little apart and far from eager to be a friend or ally to any part of the conflicted patient. Here is a stance very different from either the therapeutic alliance of modern psychoanalysis or the being and staying with the patient of existential psychiatry.

The principal tools of this ego work are three:

1. Widening and balancing, and what I have called riding the currents by transitional statements
2. The closely related double and ambiguous statements (for example, no wonder you. . . )
3. The method of successive approximations

All utilize statements, not questions or silence. All aim at eliciting truthful statements from the patient. The therapist means to give permission, draw out, and put into words what the patient has experienced, so that events can be examined as on a screen before therapist and patient. In short, this second group of techniques explores the patients' experience with the figures already displaced from medium to screen.[10] The method says, let's look at what happened. It does not promise to share the experiences, as in existential work, or explore the patient's thoughts about them, as in analysis.

Let us suppose it has already been made easier to tell the truth because the "other people" in the room have been displaced. The second group of techniques aims to reduce the intra-psychic blocks to truth-telling. In large part they disarm and recondition a defensive ego. In other language, the goal is resistance management. (Of course resistance management does not prevent the analysis of some or all resistances.)

(1) *Widening and Balancing*

Under this heading I include statements that can also be termed narrative-developing. A prototypic one is Sullivan's

10. Again I am indebted to Dr. Michael Madow for this term.

"that's amazing" or simply "amazing." The patient is invited to go on, without the therapist's having issued either a command ("tell me more") or an inquiry ("what else happened?"); a command seems authoritarian and a question inquisitive. The use of a simple descriptive word or exclamation at once indicates the listener's interest and more specifically, touches the narrative stream in such a way as to avoid obstructions.[11]

The proportion of these two, interest and guidance, will vary, depending on the character of the narrator. For example, hysterical people as a rule need from others no sign of heightened interest; on the contrary, it is astonishing how interesting they feel in the absence of any feedback at all. With these patients remarks indicating general interest will give way to signs of the specific character of our interest, that is remarks guiding the stream (unless the therapeutic purpose is to encourage fantasy formation). On the other hand, schizoid people will need signs of considerable general interest, what is called encouragement. Furthermore, specific efforts to guide the flow are not possible when the schizoid process is so powerful as to let out little material to be guided.

The ideal statement of this kind incorporates interest and guidance in a single exclamation: no other influences are brought to bear on the narrative beside those specifically selected (ambiguous statements, in contrast, mean to draw out rather than move along). This element of economy is particularly important when the narrative stream is running well but the patient is sensitive and distractible.

The guiding or obstruction-avoiding component of these brief interventions is the most difficult. In the case of Sullivan's "that's amazing" he feared the patient's stopping short of a full development of the theme (his marvelous friend) because there

11. Compare the devices "straight men" use to develop a narrative flow, for example, Watson's comments during Holmes' accounts. Watson's most successful interventions are purely exclamatory. When he asks questions, the flow stops and Holmes generally rebukes him for stupidity.

were conflicting feelings toward the friend. For that reason the patient's initial statement was challenged; the patient was asked to defend it. Unchallenged, the flow might have petered out as the opposing current pressed against it. We can theorize that by challenging the initial current himself, Sullivan diminished the need of the opposing current to make itself felt, just as I have suggested that speaking for paranoid inclinations often diminishes them. We can theorize further that speaking for the opposing current temporarily diminishes but also brings the current closer to consciousness, which, of course, Sullivan wanted eventually to accomplish.

Here are other exclamations, with corresponding obstructions that each might guide the narrative past. These few examples no more than start a grammar of such interventions.

1. "How awful!"—May prevent the patient's feeling he has overstated the problem or that the listener would play it down; this intervention counterprojects an image of therapist as unfeeling.

2. "Unbelievable."—Both challenges and empathizes. The manner in which this is said will determine how much disbelief and how much empathy are conveyed. The two obstructions foreseen are those the first-mentioned exclamations ("amazing" and "awful") are separately intended to avoid.

3. "Great".—Said directly after the patient's account of something he or she has done, it is directly encouraging. The purpose is to put down any inward or projected criticism of the act. Said sarcastically after the patient's description of something someone else has done, it would place the therapist squarely against the other person; it is then counterprojective. The feared obstruction is any tendency the patient has to identify the therapist with the other person and then to feel criticized by both.

All these guide currents. I have used the term transitional statements for efforts to *substitute* one current for another. One purpose of this substitution may also be to avoid blocks, but the main purpose is to develop conflicting currents.

I have already presented Sullivan's division of transitional statements into smooth, accented, and abrupt. We can make another division that sheds more light on the dynamics of transitional statements. This will also foreshadow a little the rationale of interpersonal therapy.

I have used the expression, wearing away the conflict. Three types of transitional statements occur, each of which wears away the conflict or increases integration differently. The three are confrontational, contrapuntal, and comparative statements.

1. *Confrontational Statements*. These oppose one line of discussion against another: "Well, is it possible that you can think of nothing he ever did that was at least unfortunate in its effect?" Hopefully, the opposing current—his perfect friend—had been sufficiently defended. Hopefully, too, enough criticism of his friend will in turn allow the value of the friendship to emerge. (In this social, experiential psychiatry it does not suffice to say we praise because we fear to hate, or hate because we fear to love: experience must have evoked the loving and the hating.) The conflict is worn away, in a particular sense: the friend was at first white, then black, then whitish, then darkish, finally gray. Where conflict was, there will be normal ambivalence.

Often confrontations and counterprojective statements are combined. "Father sounds difficult" both removes father projections from the relationship with therapist and begins wearing away the denial of the actual experiences with father. This is a more familiar use of the term "wearing away": not a wearing down of extremes to means, as just recounted, but a wearing away of blocks to perception—for example, father was perfect—that are more like dams than countercurrents. Eventually the patient may see the other side of father. Then it becomes possible to move opposing currents toward an integrated view.[12]

___

12. This is a sounder end point than commonly suggested: first patients blame their parents, then they come to understand and appreciate them.

2. *Contrapuntal statements.* These develop separate, uncon-
flicting themes. Something new, apparently unconnected occurs
in the conversation. Is the patient dissociated or is the connecting element obscure or overlooked? It would be disturbing to
inquire, even if the patient knew. Instead the new element is
mentioned again, this time by the therapist, and a narrative
flow begun. If the obscurity persists, we may be in touch with a
dissociated part. Then the therapeutic goal is not a wearing
away but a bringing together. The therapeutic device will be
transitional statements that bridge; is it possible to connect the
dissociated current to the rest of the person? There are likely to
be blocks, opposing forces, keeping the elements apart. In that
case confrontational statements may be called for, or:

3. *Comparative statements.* These point out similarities: "No
wonder you fight with your wife; she sounds like your mother." Transference interpretations are a class of these: "I remind
you of your mother." The goal is to connect and in the moment
of connection separate: "I only *seem* like your mother."

Careful selection of the linking phrase, "sound like" "remind," is important. Each time a comparison is made, there is
the opportunity to load it with different amounts of reality.
This can be critical to managing a defensive ego. To say, "Your
wife is so like your mother" (as opposed to "sounds like" or
"seems like") supports the unconscious equation of the two; it
does not attempt yet to correct it. Again, the goal is not to fight
the resistances, but to first acknowledge them.

Once mother and wife are seen as alike—now consciously—
their different features will appear. Then the separation begins.
Therapists are often wise to go on supporting the identity,
however, even after the patient questions it, until confident the
resistances have relaxed their hold.

A weak linking phrase, for example, "might be like," appeals
to the rational, skeptical ego, but invites discussion, even de-
bate; the extreme point could be a question: Is your wife like

your mother? The patient is invited to think it over. I suspect such an effort of thought would be principally useful when the patient insisted wife and and mother were alike (not when the conviction operated unconsciously). Then the weak linking phrase or question would serve as transition to discussing their differences.

"They sound so much alike" will have different impacts depending upon what word is emphasized. Emphasis on *sound* suggests they are not alike. Emphasis on *so* or *so much* does the opposite. Another determinant of the statement's impact is the strength of the patient's unconscious current. If this is petering out or has turned up opposing memories, "They sound so much alike" may be understood to suggest the opposite; it is as if the patient then will supply the emphasis on "sound." In contrast, if the current is running strong and full, the statement may be reacted to as to a supportive exclamation.

The basic purpose of comparative statements is to link phenomena (often previously developed contrapuntally) for the purpose of altering that linkage. These statements serve as transition points to such currents as these: "they aren't really alike; I shouldn't treat them the same;" (or) "they are really alike; how come I always pick people like that;" (or) "mother has dominated my life; I don't like that" etc. As is so characteristic of this method the goal is not insight. Insight is seen as merely a sign of some ego process that may reflect a fresh fiction or manipulation of the clinical relationship; at its best the insight only signals a change in the balance of internal forces; the mother introject may have retreated. Therapists' enthusiasm for the insight can bring the mother-introject back in full force: "mother always was delighted when I agreed with her." What really matters is the patient's behavior: does he treat his wife the same (or) stop picking people like that (or) stand up to his mother?

*Ambiguous and double statements*

The essential features of these have already been discussed. The goals are respectively projection-development and conflict-management. Both are most useful in clouded and conflictual situations.

The idea of ambiguous statements contradicts the usual interpersonal purpose of controlling projections. Ambiguous statements resemble the psychoanalytic screen (developing transference phenomena) or projective tests (providing an ambiguous stimulus to surface unconscious phenomena). But they are considerably more restricted in application than either of these. Like double statements, they are utilized in dangerously conflictual situations where therapists' encouragement of one element or other of antagonistic currents might disrupt the relationship. In other words, they are needed in precariously *balanced* situations.

Ambiguous statements provide material easily ignored. Placed among the indifferent material are words that could be taken up by one or more of the patient's conflicting forces. The purpose of ambiguous statements, however, is not to emphasize the significant words. If the balance of the patient's internal forces is such as to take up one or another theme—all right. The point is, not to throw the therapist's weight too much in one direction or another. This might provoke a violent reaction. "Surely, and who knows how sure one can be when mother criticizes; and then of course others criticize *her*." (Which, if either, element will the patient take up—mother's criticizing him or his criticizing mother?)

I have emphasized already the precarious balance of forces characteristic of schizophrenic patients' attitudes toward their parents. Powerful forces and aggressive currents, on the one hand, stand shackled by internalized parental attitudes on the other. Support for either side provokes powerful reactions from the other. Ambiguous statements explore what elements are most available for discussion. Once surfaced, however, a single current in acute schizophrenic people can seldom be explored alone. Double statements are needed; that is, the other side of the conflict must be acknowledged. "She's a pain, although I suppose she has her good side." (In existential work, by way of contrast, seemingly irresolvable conflicts are handled by placing oneself within, e.g. empathizing with the feeling of dilemma. "There is no place to go." Once within the dilemma the existential therapist looks around, as it were, for ways out.) Interpersonal technique works from outside: the contending elements are edged bit by bit into view, for example, "I hate her" and "I love and fear her." By being in view I mean describing on the screen before therapist and patient the experiences grounding each side of the conflict, for example, "she kept me at home so I didn't learn to dance" and "I felt protected," on the other side. When hate has been opposed by fear rather than love (when the home has been a concentration camp), the point of conflict-resolution will not be ambivalence but rejection. Therapists will have to acknowledge that there are human situations about which nothing good can be said.

### The technique of successive approximations

This is the principal interpersonal technique for extending a narrative in directions the patient does not undertake spontaneously. (It corresponds, on the factual level, to the emotional extensions, through hypothetical statements—Havens, 1976—by which existential method explores the inner, phenomenological world.) Essentially the therapist makes statements of "fact" ("mother was difficult"), put down for correction.

As a rule, one overshoots or undershoots. The patient responds, "this, not that." The therapist makes another statement; the patient a counterstatement. The truth is gradually, dialectically approached.

The technique of successive approximations has three advantages over questions and silence. It gives permission to speak of difficult matters, by example. It puts into words many things patients need to talk about that they may never have verbalized. Finally, it facilitates looking at events. A statement of events puts the subject out there. Questions, in contrast, direct attention to the questioned or to the questioner; silence throws the patient back on himself.

Many therapists unpracticed in the technique will have difficulty making statements that are little more than guesses; the initial irresistible temptation will be to turn them into questions. There will also be considerable initial fear of "leading the witness," especially suggestible and obedient witnesses. Some will want to diminish this occurrence by liberal use of maybe, perhaps, and may and might. With more confidence in the method, however, statements will be made at a later time contradicting those agreed with earlier; this is an easy check for excessive suggestibility and obedience. If patients agree with both statements, it is best to avoid calling attention to the contradictions, which can be humiliating. Bridging statements can resolve the problem: "sometimes it seems so-and-so, sometimes the opposite" (a version of "consistency is the hobgoblin of small minds"). One can then explore counterprojectively and by the method of successive approximations the patient's agreeableness: "Father couldn't take no for an answer," etc. The purpose is to get the facts, and also now a therapeutic purpose, learning to tell the truth to someone who can take no for an answer.[13]

13. Many others, besides those already acknowledged, work in the ways just outlined. Bibring (1954) described manipulation as "the employment of various emotional systems existing in the patient for the purpose of achieving therapeutic change": the present book could be characterized as an exposition of that statement. The gestaltists often work counterprojectively: by saying "pretend I'm your father" they imply "I'm really not." Cooper (1971) writes of therapy as "depopulation," getting rid of the "other people in the room." Haley and Hoffman (1967) and Minuchin (1974) have recently developed aspects of the interpersonal approach. Bateson (Bateson, Jackson, Haley, Weakland, 1956) is an important theoretician of the school. Fairbairn (1963), working from Klein's observations and intuitions, has provided perhaps the most complete development of the concepts of introjection and projection.

# SEVEN

# Therapeutic Rationale

IT IS EASY TO BELIEVE these counterprojective techniques reduce projection. It is not so easy to believe they comprise a full-fledged therapeutic method. Of course, no therapeutic method is completely self-sufficient. Nondirective counseling is not always nondirective. Probably no psychoanalysis has ever been conducted without using some of the parameters of analysis. But both these methods have been explored in extended treatment settings.

I also may not be wise to describe participant observation as a separate method. In the sectarian wilderness of contemporary psychiatry we should move toward togetherness, not separateness; students and practitioners are bewildered enough. Nevertheless, it seems to me we must clarify the methods even at the cost of separating them for a while. Only in this way can they be developed, tested, and their indications and contraindications discovered. Of course the goal is not to use one method always or only.

I will discuss the therapeutic rationale of interpersonal method under three headings, which describe roughly successive phases of the work: displacing, reducing, and relearning. I will contrast these with the principal phases of psychoanalytic work, developing and working through the transference neurosis, and, to a lesser extent, with those I have described for existential therapy, feeling understood, gaining connectedness, themes and confrontations, and leaving behind (Havens, in press). There is much overlap both among phases and among the methods. Again, my goal is not to build fences but to sharpen techniques.

## DISPLACING

Freud's formulation of his final theory of instincts rendered possible the adoption of a psychopathology in which a definite role could be assigned to aggression as well as to libido; and, for another, Freud's subsequent formulation of his theory of the mental constitution in terms of id, ego and superego promoted the development of an ego-psychology based largely upon the conception of an internal object-relationship, involving aggressive no less than libidinal components, between the ego and the superego. These developments enabled Freud to envisage the possibility of a sadistic superego assuming the role of an internal parental moral persecutor, and to recognize that it actually assumed this role in cases of depression. Subsequently, the researches of Melanie Klein led her to the conclusion that the development of the superego is effected through the integration, to any degree of success, of a multiplicity of internalized part objects, many of which are "bad objects" and function as internal persecutors. In accordance with this view, it becomes possible to understand how, in circumstances favouring regression, the superego may disintegrate into the internalized part objects from which it originated, with the consequent release of a host of internal persecutors, and how such internal persecutors may be defensively projected into the external world. (Fairbairn, 1956)

The movement of projections out of the medium between therapist and patient and onto the screen before them is as fundamental to the interpersonal management of the regressive situation Fairbairn describes as the provision of a neutral screen on the therapist is to psychoanalytic treatment. We can say that each provides the respective operating theatre for therapeutic work.

In play therapy, as in interpersonal therapy, projections are dealt with "out there"; the gain is that of concreteness in the miniature world of play objects and the loss that of the subtlety and variety and therefore reality verbal representations provide.[1] (Some of the concreteness of play therapy can be recaptured for interpersonal method by referring to the figures—introjects—mentioned as "sitting over there," perhaps at the same time pointing to a chair.)[2] Group therapy combines features of both interpersonal and psychoanalytic work: from the standpoint of the group leader many of the projections occur out there; others land on him. Of course he cannot move the other group members here and there as he might play objects, but what he loses in control he gains, or more than gains, in the power of group feelings and interactions. Nor does the group situation prevent the leader from being analytic, existential, or the participant observer.

Bowen has developed techniques for training patients to deal directly with their parents (Bowen, 1972), to correct parataxic distortions or transferences by interaction with the parents themselves. This puts the projections at the furthest point out there. Existential work is at the opposite pole. When therapists are able to be and stay with their parents, in principle nothing is projected; there are no screens. When the existential therapist says, "it is frightening to hate," the fear and hatred are shared, not displaced.

What are the therapeutic reasons to displace projections?

1. The most obvious is to escape paranoid projection. As hostile feelings settle more and more on the therapist, the whole

---

1. Play therapy can be either interpersonal or psychoanalytic in its emphasis, that is the therapist can say: "mother is tall" or let the child express its fantasy.

2. This was Susan Miller-Havens', R.N., suggestion and recent experience.

treatment effort is endangered. Interpretations are not only fu-
tile but hazardous; no matter how tactfully couched, they are
too easily seen as accusations, adding to the hostile feelings.
Questions are as bad, because they convey inquisitiveness,
snoopiness. Nor is it usually safe to move closer to the patient
as part of an existential effort. This increases any homosexual
excitement, making the hostile distancing more necessary.
Counterprojective statements, on the other hand, quickly re-
store a therapeutic atmosphere.

As suggested, the stronger the paranoid feelings, the more
vigorous must be the counterprojective statement. This is no
time for bland, neutral, or even friendly comments. As a result,
therapists making vigorous counterprojective statements appear hostile, sarcastic; a sensitive observer will protest that the
patient is being attacked. It is not, however, the patient who is
being attacked but the projected introjects. This is the reason
the patient feels less hostile, less attacked, after properly aimed
counterprojective statements. [3]

Of course, a patient does not have to be chronically paranoid
to precipitate paranoid clinical situations. No long-term relationship is without them. Moreover, as Searles has shown,
therapists often are the ones precipitating suspiciousness by
their own hostility (1965). As a result counterprojective technique is useful no matter what the diagnosis or the main clinical
instrument being utilized.

So-called borderline and narcissistic character disorders,
whether overtly paranoid or not, provide another frequent occasion for counterprojective work. In these cases the target is
"great expectations." Unless these are controlled, they may
hypertrophy and then collapse sharply at the first break in therapeutic perfection. (Some therapists live and work off great expectations and expect to be dropped when their imperfections

---

3. Patients can learn to deal with their own hostilely projecting relatives and associates in the same
way. A wife, endlessly criticized by her husband, may find it a great relief to talk about the husband's
mother, *not*, however, to call attention to his confusion or to interpret it.

are discovered.) What needs to be counterprojected is the image of therapy itself; this must be talked about. Again, the greater the expectations the more vigorous the counterprojection needs to be: "Lord knows, how little good therapy has done anyone." Such remarks become of almost emergency importance if the patient has great expectations toward the present therapist in spite of repeated disappointments with earlier ones.

2. "The superego may disintegrate into the internalized part-object from which it originated, with the consequent release of a host of internal persecutors": When disintegration has reached acute psychotic proportions, transference is immediate and overwhelming (psychotic transference) and the patient's stream of thought dissociated. The dissociation results from the rapidly shifting internal objects; the patient experiences, and is experienced as, a babble of voices. Furthermore, "such internal persecutors may be defensively projected into the external world." The two principal psychotherapeutic tools are then existential and interpersonal methods. With existential method one attempts to place oneself in the center of the patient's experience in the hope of helping the patient reach and regroup the scattered fragments (gaining connectedness). Sometimes, however, no center can be found or the center is moving, like a tornado, at a pace faster than the therapist. In that case, one can only counterproject the fragments that appear. (Or, using commonsense terms, one avoids confirming the patient's fearful expectations.) Occasionally vigorous talking about actual figures known to be frightening results in a rapid regrouping of dissociated elements. It is as if the patient's personality were an army in retreat before some terrifying force: as soon as the terrifying force is identified and attacked, by the therapist, the patient can regroup and turn back.

In my experience dissociation seldom occurs without very obvious psychotic transference. Psychotic transference, however, commonly occurs without significant dissociation. (Indeed I believe one can identify at least glimmerings of psychotic transference in even the most classical and successful psycho-analysis.[4] Counterprojective method has therefore a much broader field of application than acute psychosis and paranoid states.

3. To what extent does the use of counterprojective statements make possible the rapid and controlled surfacing and exploration of various transference (parataxic) elements (just as a wide variety of family objects in play therapy facilitates transference work)? The main restriction must surely be the dynamic state of the patient. We do not need to subscribe to the old opinion that each memory must be recovered in the reverse order of its being laid down, or the Reichian view that one should work from the outside in, in order to accept that not every psychic element is equally available at all times. To move a projection from the medium onto the screen, it must first be present in the medium, that is it must be dynamically present in the relationship. In this matter, the only advantage that counterprojective method has over classical analytic technique is that it encourages the mention of transference figures that do not appear to be present in the relationship. These silent projections may be overlooked by all but the most intuitive analysts.

Therapists will have to balance this advantage of interpersonal method against the alleged disadvantage active therapeutic technique carries: the more active therapists are, the more individuated they become to their patients and the more restricted and specialized the target they offer the patient's projective tendencies. Silence, neutrality, out-of-sightness offer, it is alleged, the broadest and least distorting target for the unconscious psychic elements seeking a relationship. Furthermore, the classical position provides a steady base for detached scientific observation; the reactions of different patients and the same patient at different times can be measured against a relatively unchanging baseline. I write that this is an alleged advantage because I believe it has been misunderstood. In particular,

4. An adequate discussion of this would move us far beyond the scope of the present book, into, for example, the subject of "neurotic delusions."

relative silence, neutrality, out-of-sightness is itself a *very spe-cific* target. Of course the unconscious tendencies do not "see" it as a rational opportunity for their free exercise. The essence of the analytic opportunity is that the unconscious tendencies respond to the neutral analyst on the basis of their prior experiences. Silence may have meant to a particular patient kindly receptivity, but it is just as likely to have meant to another coldness, indifference, and to another indecisiveness, drift-ing etc.: thus the transference neurosis. About this line of reason-ing there is general agreement. The problem—a point so often made in these pages—is that the specificity of the analytic target restricts its use to those for whom its particular features do not constitute an overwhelming stimulus; in analytic language, those patients for whom the transference situation, as classi-cally awaited, does not precipitate a transference psychosis. I have been arguing that this limitation of the theory of analytic therapy is by no means necessary. Once admit the possibility of a whole range of therapeutic positions (which indeed occur naturally in keeping with different therapists' ideas of silence and neutrality) and of altering the therapeutic position from time to time in each case—then this range and the alterations are in the service of the development of an equal range of trans-ferences that need not fall over into psychotic transferences.

This will not convince those for whom silence and some degree of detachment are inherently less distorting and less structured stimuli than any verbal stimulus or other activity. I can only believe these therapists must have had some particular experiences in their development which have rendered silence and detachment of special value, perhaps in permitting the free play of their own thoughts and feelings. I am convinced there are others for whom the same conditions *forbid* the free play of thoughts and feelings.

I like the expressions "playing the transference" and "tuning oneself" for an active, relativistic stance toward patients' pro-jections; the goal is not to let the misunderstandings become overwhelming. I suppose role playing has been the device most often used: the patient becomes excited; the therapist is a little cooler at the door; one tunes oneself so as not to overexcite. The *verbal* devices suggested here—what I have also called counterrole playing—have the same effect. One downplays the therapy, for example, with a vivid phrase. These verbal devices have greater flexibility than the role playing ones, and appeal to those for whom play acting feels uncomfortable.

## REDUCING

As soon as significant figures have been displaced to the screen, the work of historical reconstruction can begin. In essence, pictures of events are developed by means of the statements discussed in Chapter 6. In order to reduce the patient's projective tendencies, these pictures must be detailed and eventually they must be seen in a distant perspective. The process can be compared to putting on a pair of glasses both clearer (in the sense of correcting a distorting or astigmatic tendency) and more powerful than was worn before.

Therapists starting to use these techniques will not know what statements to make. Not only will they be unaccustomed to making exclamations and assertions and fearful lest these unduly influence the patient, but they will not have in mind categories detailed enough to suggest appropriate statements (in the way that knowledge of the mental status categories and psychosexual developmental categories guide the mental status examination and free associative listening). I have found most useful *categories of everyday events*, such as meeting and parting, mealtimes and vacation times, in school and out of school, essentially when and where things happen, but on a more microscopic level than age, grade, or geographical area.[5] Here is a group of representative statements.

Weekends were worse than, very like, or better than weekdays.

5. The writings of Erving Goffman (e.g., 1975) abound in such categories.

Meeting her was all right, but then after a few days (or the reverse) . . .

You could play games together but the dinner table was difficult (or the reverse).

Right in the middle of making love something happened.

Again, the purpose of these is not to "state truths" (it is sometimes wise to get as far away as possible from the truth), but to indicate possibilities. One can compare it to making a mark; the patient responds, "not there, here." After enough marks, erasures and corrections, the picture emerges. Or, to make another comparison, each statement is like a brushstroke; it may be left to stand or be painted over, the color deepened a little or another stroke put beside it which reveals its color; again, the picture gradually emerges.

It is also necessary to gain distance from the pictures that emerge. (This is part of what is meant by mastering or possessing one's experience and of putting the past behind one.) Gaining distance is achieved by the narrative itself, that is, reconstructing the past recreates and creates the past: it becomes something we have done. The act of narration does not by itself, however, gain all the distance necessary to offset the projective tendency. The past may still, we can say, discolor the present even after a very thorough narrative. Indeed there will be parts of anyone's past that one does not want to distance; the act of narration will surface such that one will want to hold closer than before.

In order to gain adequate distance (I could speak also of a new or better perspective), I have found it necessary to counter-project both myself and the patient. Thus, although the bulk of reducing statements will concern others, some must concern therapist and patient. In this way the two are placed out there: both parties gain distance on themselves. An important therapeutic implication is conveyed by the statements about the patient. They imply: this is the way you have been; perhaps you will not want to be so much that way any longer.

The foregoing must seem very obscure to anyone who has not practiced these techniques. Here is an illustrative sequence:

PT:    My father berated me every morning if my hair wasn't combed. (PT is very dishevelled, even though he hopes to be promoted in his bank job.)

TH:    You said he would mention it even when *he* was dishevelled. (TH is distancing himself from father in preparation for what is to follow. That is, he cannot usefully confront PT with his self-destructive behavior if he is at all confused with father: PT would then become more dishevelled.)

PT:    I remember once he was drunk in the morning—he still said it.

TH:    The bank people probably aren't drunk but they don't sound much better. (TH also needs to separate himself from the bank people, since they too have criticized PT's appearance.

PT:    Actually, I like my boss.

TH:    Well, I can picture *some* bankers' reaction to long hair. (The goal of this is to have PT "picture" himself being reacted to by a banker.)

Note that this last statement is a confrontation. More specifically the patient is being confronted with himself, just as all along this method has been confronting him with his realistic past. (Psychoanalysis, in contrast, aims to confront patients with their fantasies, and existential work makes confrontation with the self comparatively safe.) By working on the screen, as opposed to on the patient, painful remarks will not be experienced so directly. Counterprojective technique also makes it possible for the therapist to separate himself from the confronting remark, as in the example: the bankers confront the patient, not the therapist. I have found this method permits a much greater use of the Reichian characterological confrontations than is possible without it. As a result, interpersonal method has a large place in the therapy of character problems, what Ferenczi called the "secret psychoses."

Similarly, remarks about therapy and therapist will help displace these too, a desirable step especially in termination. At that point patients need to gain distance on therapy; this must be put behind them as well. Otherwise, both the patient's view of therapy and of himself tend to petrify into a fixed, final shape, the "numbing feeling of reality," with loss of perspective or distance.

The basic operational plan behind reducing is very like the plan of psychoanalytic working through. At first glance the two do not look alike. In psychoanalysis the infantile neurosis is surfaced and repeatedly interpreted in the transference; meanwhile the resistances, coming from the ego, are interpreted; and both infantile cathexes and ego resistances are again and again brought into consciousness along with their roots in the past. The implication is: This is the way you act because of old wishes and the way things were.

In participant observation, transference phenomena are also surfaced but immediately and not onto the therapist but in front of both patient and therapist. Projective responses are then reduced. In the psychoanalytic working through process, attention is called to the difference between fantasy and reality: "You feel about me the way you did about mother." The goal is insight into the power of old wishes and fantasies. By means of the various reducing statements, on the other hand, the past is illuminated out there: "that is the way it was." Of course the most obvious difference is the emphasis, in the case of analysis, on wishes and fantasies (and in theory, on instincts) and, in the case of interpersonal work, on life experiences and reactions to it (and in theory on behavioral learning). Neither denies the importance of the other (though there is disagreement about the

place of instinct): One says—what did you think?, the other—
what happened?

Fantasy will emerge spontaneously; it is not likely to emerge
any other way: hence free associative method. The realistic
past, however, does not emerge spontaneously: hence the use
of narrative-developing statements. (For the sake of simplicity I
am avoiding a further comparison, with existential work, in
which the central question is "How did it feel?")

It is often claimed that interpersonal work deals more with
the present than does psychoanalysis. In fact analysis is also
very concerned with the present. The working through process
depends upon old fantasies occurring again and again in the
present and being interpreted there. On the other hand, if the
real past is not illuminated by interpersonal method, little that
the patient does in the present makes sense. The pattern of behavior can be identified and its self-fulfilling aspects clarified,
and the two at least attenuated, but the success of that alone
(without a simultaneous surfacing of the past) must depend
upon the power of the therapist. It is really the therapist's word
against the patient's, the old suggestion therapy revisited. This
is so because to the extent that the patient actually perceives the
present through the lenses of the past (which is to say no more
than that his behavior is learned), he can only change his
behavior if he first changes his perception. If he changes his behavior without changing his perception, he is assuming someone else's perception of the world. There is a therapeutic school
that aims to change behavior first and let the perception catch
up. The difficulty with this is its outright authoritarianism: the
patients have to accept these therapists' perceptions of the
world.[6]

To repeat, psychoanalysis and interpersonalism do not differ
in their emphasis on past or present. They differ in their
emphasis on fantasy and reality and in the operations by which

6. Interpersonal method can also be authoritarian, especially when the technique of successive
approximation is used to approximate the therapist's reality and not the patient's. But then one also
encounters authoritarian analysts: "this is what you are really thinking."

the two are surfaced and affected. Both have to develop and work through their respective materials.

Interpersonal workers in the reducing phase assume that projection is a learned behavior and can be unlearned. In the simplest theory projections are assumed to reproduce previous experiences; thus Schreber's hallucinations and delusions can be understood as essential memories of his father's treatment of him. In its more sophisticated form (as in the writings of Fairbairn), part-objects are internalized (essentially, learned), may function as internal persecutors and be projected onto the external world.[7] With either formulation, the historical reconstruction and distancing of the reducing process move either the memories or the introjects from their place in the intrapsychic unconscious back to conscious experience. Seeing the world as it was opens the way to seeing it a different way, to a perceptual relearning, which is the final phase of the work. In different language, unconscious or barely conscious attitudes (e.g., people are untrustworthy) are realized ("I see now that my world did appear arbitrary and unreasonable") which in turn suggests other possibilities.

## RELEARNING

I will argue that interpersonal therapy is behavioristic. Its success depends upon training, not upon insight or feeling or the treatment of a disease entity. Pathological responses are to be reshaped or extinguished by the therapist's behavior. This is a social, perceptual behaviorism.

The assumptions of the method are three. First, it is assumed that projections reflect critical psychopathology; projection

7. The theory of projection is today a great muddle. For example, see the very different views of the Schreber materials held by Niederland (1960) who takes the more traditional Freudian position, and Schatzman (1973) who is closer to a learning position. There is also disagreement as to whether introjects enter into the ego as well as the superego. I believe they do. The work of Hendrick (1942) and Modell (1968) seems to me decisive.

occupies as prominent a place in this work as repression does in psychoanalysis. Second, it is assumed that counterprojective remarks can bring the projections out of the relationship and into the discussion; talking about the projections constitutes the "fundamental rule" of participant observation. Finally, it is assumed that projections can be extinguished in the course of a relationship; patients can learn fresh responses either to fresh projections or perhaps to a social field free of projections.

The essence of this viewpoint is that people act as they do because of their perceptions of the social situation. The essence of the treatment theory, in turn, is manipulation or correction of these perceptions. Behavior is to be affected through changes in social perception (by destroying the social fantasy systems).[8]

It is still not clear, however, why "seeing the world as it was" changes social perception. I have suggested a series of steps leading from unconscious attitudes and social fantasy systems to an awareness of the experiences shaping those attitudes. But how are the attitudes or fantasy systems themselves to change? So long as the patient selects or brings about those stimuli that reinforce his learned view of the world, he cannot change. To the extent that he responds to other stimuli he has already changed. How are the other stimuli to be perceived?

Behaviorists have given the most direct answer. In the principal forms of modern experimental behaviorism, behavior is

8. Compare this with Alexander's account of what he called the corrective emotional experience. "In the formulation of the dynamics of treatment, the usual tendency is to stress the repetition of the old conflict in the transference relationship and to emphasize the similarity of the old conflict situation to the transference situation. The therapeutic significance of the differences between the original conflict situation and the present therapeutic situation is often overlooked. And in just this difference lies the secret of the therapeutic value of the analytic procedure. Because the therapist's attitude is different from that of the authoritative person of the past, he gives the patient an opportunity to face again, under more favorable circumstances, those emotional situations which were formerly unbearable and to deal with them in a manner different from the old" (Alexander, 1961).

This is essentially role playing in a psychoanalytic setting. It differs from what I have been describing in two respects. In interpersonal method the projections (or transference) are managed, not by role playing, but by counterprojective and other statements. In addition, emphasis falls on the actual figures in the patient's life, not as in Alexander's technique, on the therapist's behavior.

the critical datum, rather than perception. It is the patients' behavior that is to be changed by various conditioning procedures. Nevertheless, behavior depends upon perception; something must go into as well as come out of the organism; or, in the language of behaviorism, there are stimuli as well as responses. When we speak of changes in perception, we could as well be speaking of changes in stimuli. And, of course, all we know objectively about others' perception is whatever manifests itself in behavior.

Behavior therapy can be said to work through perception. When a phobic stimulus loses its power to evoke pathological behavior, it is being reperceived. There are two lines of indirect evidence for this: the same stimulus then evokes a different response and the stimulus may appear different to the patient. (Again, of course, behaviorists do not talk this way because perception is a subjective response.)

My point is that the treatment rationale of participant observation can be put in fully behavioral terms. Patients and therapist together gradually approach the original, anxiety-provoking stimuli that have been projected onto the therapist and then displaced to the screen. The anxiety and resulting defensive operations provoked by these stimuli are gradually extinguished insofar as they are not reinforced. Adequate anxiety management prevents the reinforcement. Relearning therefore occurs in the process of displacing and reducing. [9]

9. Counterprojective behavior can thus be said to reconstruct the stimulus world of the present. One major point of difference among modern psychotherapists is the extent to which the reconstruction should take place in memory or in actuality. Bowen (1972) for example, encourages dealing directly with remaining family figures; others go to the opposite extreme. Workers like Novey (1968) fall in between.

# EIGHT

# Termination

I WILL PRESENT a theoretical structure for termination in interpersonal terms and contrast it with the more extensively studied concepts of psychoanalytic and existential termination. The value of this structure is heuristic: it can guide research by suggesting certain observations and experiments which in turn will modify the structure.

Therapy stops because either conditions make going on impossible or the work is done. Termination is also, however, an event in the therapeutic process offering its own opportunities and difficulties. The discussion that follows is organized around three major opportunities of termination and their attendant difficulties. I have termed the three opportunities *reviving and reliving*, *surviving discontinuity*, and *gaining perspective on therapist and therapy*.

## REVIVING AND RELIVING

Termination is a unique event in the therapeutic process because it represents a threat and an intention before it occurs, a loss when it occurs, and a sharp discontinuity after it has occurred. Therefore, one important aspect of termination is its ability to mobilize memories and feelings attached to earlier threats, intentions, losses, and discontinuities. While this is true whatever the therapeutic approach, each of the principal approaches explores a different aspect of this termination opportunity.

It is characteristic of interpersonal work to externalize the memories. By this I mean locating the problematic aspect of the termination experience outside the patient (by such a familiar remark as "Mother may not have warned you when she planned to leave"). The patient is not asked to take responsibility for his experience, on the assumption that his knowledge and power in the early family were small. The externalization is meant to recognize that situation.

It is the situation that is recognized, not the patient's wishes, fantasies, or feelings, as in psychoanalytic or existential work. One advantage is that the patient is not made responsible for what he may not have been responsible for. One disadvantage is that the patient's own part in whatever happened is put aside. When that must be dealt with, any expectation of *not* being held responsible, which has been reinforced by the whole interpersonal position, will have to be counterprojected in turn, for a start perhaps by, "It seems that no one gives you credit for anything!"

The patient's experience of intentionality could be pursued along similar lines: "They said one thing and did another." Such a remark could not only surface the patient's experience of family intention, it could also prepare him better for termination. Perhaps we do not know what the patient thinks of the termination plans. Associative material may not clarify the matter. Existential sharing of aroused anger or sadness may not either. Perhaps the patient has failed to take seriously the announcement of termination on the basis of experience with significant adults who did not mean what they said. The associative material may reveal this, as might a lack of feeling uncovered existentially. But perhaps neither do. The patient must then be surprised when the termination actually occurs. Moreover, the termination work will have been done superficially if at all.

Note again the fictive attitude implied. Therapist's remarks are not more accepted at face value by the patient than are the patient's by the therapist. Each must be explored counter-projectively.

The value of this fictive attitude is nowhere more evident than in termination. Perhaps every therapist has wondered to what extent the feelings and fantasies mobilized on termination are related to transference and to what extent to the loss of actual features of the therapist himself. Plainly, working through the one need not include working through the other. Indeed, with prolonged therapeutic relationships one encounters transference material used as a defense against feelings for the therapist ("I don't love you, I still love my father"). Complete termination depends upon working out both components. I will discuss shortly the means by which interpersonal technique facilitates gaining realistic perspective on therapist and therapy. Suffice it to say, counterprojective remarks induce sharp, often brief, drops in transference projection. Then one can note what other feelings remain.

By contrast, sharing the experience of threat, loss, or whatever and extending these experiences by mention of earlier ones—such are the staples of existential termination. Reviving and reliving are achieved through the sharing and extending; one seeks to be with the patients where they are—in the wonderfully concrete language of existential work. Separation of past and present is not made interpretatively or counterprojectively. The existential point is to experience, not talk about (in keeping with the existential avoidance of subject-object splits). Past and present are separated experientially: pastness and presentness are different feeling states and can be shared as such between patient and doctor. A prototypic statement might be: "Loving (hating) me now may someday feel like loving (hating) them then." Similarly, separating feelings for the parents from feelings for the therapist depends upon the gradual refinement of each; the further one moves into either, the more likely one is to find differences between the two and with these differences, specific experiences of loss. In short, existential workers seek as deeply and widely as possible to be with their patients in the experience of termination, to be with them in the loss of the therapist as much as in the loss of the parents. The existential equivalent to transference interpretation is the gradually felt difference between the two loss experiences.

In psychoanalysis the transference neurosis describes the repressed wishes now brought out of repression onto the person of the therapist (from repression to projection). Some would broaden the meaning of transference neurosis to include all feelings attached to the therapist whether repressed or not; others would restrict it to the oedipal transference neurosis. In either case, the fresh attachment of wishes is itself a revival. As the wishes are bit by bit interpreted, the memories and feelings associated with them are experienced: this is the reliving.

Termination is foreshadowed in every transference interpretation. Whenever the analyst interprets the transference, he separates himself a little from the earlier figures in whose place he is being loved. In this sense interpretations are intended to be counterprojective; but to what extent they succeed depends upon how persuasive their content is to the patient and how much or little their form matches the behavior of the parent figures; for example, if both analyst and parent sound whiny or critical, the interpretation will reinforce, not reduce, the transference neurosis. Nevertheless, the purpose of transference interpretation is to terminate the transference, and when this is completed, the main work of analysis is done.

Almost every analysis demonstrates, however, that matters are not so simple. Instead of termination signaling the end of the transference neurosis, commonly it spurs its revival. Forces nicely ordered seem once again active, even rampant. Hopefully, this revival is a last gasp, a terminal convulsion, but that, too, is seldom wholly the case. Instead, the analyst discovers that the particular features of termination have brought out of repression wishes and experiences not previously encountered.

This exemplifies a great problem of psychoanalytic method. The blank screen is an invitation to project, but it is rarely a *carte blanche*. The most powerful forces that emerge may do so not in response to therapeutic anonymity and neutrality but to the actual characteristics of the analyst, for example, his sex, height, or the paintings on his wall. This is most evident when a second analysis revives some aspect of the patient's neurosis only hinted at in the first.

It is an unsettled question as to which favors the richest transference development: a more anonymous or a more actual presentation of the therapist. Perhaps there is a similarity to the difference between material produced by the Rorschach Test, on the one hand, and the Thematic Apperception Test, on the other, the one a relatively unstructured, unrealistic set of stimuli, the other very definitely structured and particularized. Psychologists secure very interesting responses to both. Can we speak of one being more fundamental than the other?

In the most austere analysis, theoretically there is no real analyst to terminate with; everything takes place at the level of transference. Even in this hypothetical instance, however, the objectivity and rationality of the procedure lie outside the transference neurosis; the patient must relate to these qualities as realities. Typically, psychoanalytic writers see this relationship as one of identification: the patient makes objectivity and rationality part of himself. In such a case there would be no need to terminate with these aspects of the analyst. The patient could keep them always.

## SURVIVING DISCONTINUITY

*I wanted the moments of my life to follow*
*and order themselves like those of a life remembered.*
*You might as well try and catch time by the tail.*

*Sartre, Nausee*

I have used the word *discontinuity* rather than *loss* because the rupture which is termination makes possible a larger victory than simply surviving the loss of a particular object. Ideally, termination provides the opportunity to confront and survive the random, unpredictable, discontinuous nature of living human experience. This is very different from the settled expectation that one loses and hopefully works through one's losses.

It is existential workers who have highlighted the unpredictable, even absurd quality of human life: only in retrospect, they argue, can human experience be ordered and understood; the very act of examining, understanding, collating experience stops life in its tracks, producing a whole new set of unpredictable consequences. Even those parts of the future we can predict are not fixed in their human significance. Knowing they will occur introduces a new dimension to our relationship with them: shall we welcome these predictable events, plan for them, curse or avoid them? In short, as soon as we anticipate something, we render our relationship with it unpredictable. For example, when the event occurs, we may discover we overestimated our pleasure in it, and be disappointed, or the reverse.

Existential workers have also provided the most direct assistance with this discontinuous nature of human experience. Being with the patient in the experience of discontinuity, sharing the existential *angst*, not only provides companionship for the sufferer in dread, it makes available an identification with one who can bear the dread, if the therapist can. Thus, the capacity for bearing fear (and grief, fury, and joy as well) may be strengthened.

Counterprojective method approaches the phenomenon of discontinuity indirectly, through its opposite. This is the expectation of *continuity*, what are sometimes called great or narcissistic expectations, for example, that life will continue uninterrupted, that one will be provided with love, etc. Of course the boundary between realistic and unrealistic expectations is uncertain; cheerful people do not put it where cynics do. It is also uncertain the extent to which unrealistic expectations are a necessary component of the normal personality (witness Eugene O'Neill's "life is made tolerable by illusions") or to what extent unrealistic expectations are useful as a self-fulfilling mechanism ("the power of positive thinking"). But almost everyone agrees that some expectations are more realistic than others, that some are even great or very unrealistic expectations. We encounter the latter in many character disorders (today a term very broadly applied), manic and hypomanic personalities, many hysterical and dependent people, and the iatrogenic phenomenon in which the therapist has promised or appeared to promise more than could be delivered. The last is a large body of cases worthy of the detailed attention Searles has given the comparable *hostility* in therapists.

It is worth noting, too, that some investigators, preeminently Binswanger, have assigned false expectations the major role in neurosis-formation (what could be termed the narcissistic core of neurosis). Binswanger suggested that a phobia, for example, is pathological because the patient refuses to accept the inherently fearful nature of life. We should *all* fear, he implied, because life is dangerous. For the phobic person the truth about life has broken through in only a small part of his world picture, the phobic object. Study the rest of the phobic person's world view, it is said, and its otherwise unrealistic perspective will come clear. The job of treatment then is to learn to bear the fear, not abolish it.

Because expectations are interpersonal phenomena—that is, expectations of others—they can also be dealt with counterprojectively. Put differently, expectations are projections; they can be detached from the speaker by counterprojective remarks.

What follows is a group of such remarks, intended to make explicit and gradually bring under control great expectations. Of course their specific content must be a function of the patients' specific dynamics. The examples illustrate only some formal possibilities.

PT:   The fee is too high. (Actually the fee was small, but PT wanted to continue treatment without paying.)

TH:   Especially in view of your own heavy expenses elsewhere. (This is existential, deepening their shared experience of PT's sense of deprivation. The sharing, however, is just a way station toward the great expectations.)

PT:   I need the treatment. (This is probably true, but not what PT means. He means he needs the treatment free.)

TH:   But how often it has disappointed you. (I.e., "Even when the doctors are paid, they don't help much." Still largely existential, the remark moves toward the counterprojection "Let us talk about those people who disappoint you.")

PT:   I really want it to succeed. (Again both a plea and a threat.)

TH:   Hope springs eternal. (A far cry from existential because PT is not hoping but *warning*; TH is the one to whom the job of being hopeful and effective has been delegated. "Hope springs eternal" means "don't put me among the hoping ones." The delegation is refused.)

PT:   Do you think I'm hopeless? ("I expect you to give me hope.")

TH:   God, I hope not. (Again counterprojective, this time against two likely projections: "The doctor doesn't care about me" and "He should do the hoping and sustaining for both of us." The double counterprojection says "I care about you, but can't carry the load by myself." Why not say this directly? Because it would make explicit and debatable matters still largely outside awareness. The goal of this work is not awareness but clearing the projections.)

So far two types of counterprojective remarks have been illustrated: one to offset the patient's delegation of responsibility to the therapist, the other to offset what declining that responsibility will precipitate, anger with the therapist. Note how the dialogue develops through the successive counterprojective remarks.

PT:  My father doesn't lift a finger.

TH:  You'd expect him to. No wonder you look so hard for help elsewhere. (These sentences counterproject, first, an earlier figure upon whom PT may have been justified in placing some expectations. Secondly, TH ducks away from the load understandably ("no wonder") displaced onto him. The great expectations are being made more and more explicit, not in relation to TH but "out there.")

PT:  I feel empty and half dead.

TH:  They seem to promise so much and deliver so little. (Now both expectations and disappointments are made explicit. This double statement surfaces both currents at once, allowing the patient to develop whichever he wants and also to feel that each justifies the other. Moreover, it points toward a future opportunity, the possible refusion of split good and bad objects.)

Here are two more examples:

PT:  I feel helpless.

TH:  You are.

PT:  If this is the way it is, I'd like to quit and never commit myself.

TH:  That's what a lot of people decide.

I have drawn both these exchanges out of contexts that made clear the patient was threatening. In each case the threat was also a projection onto the therapist of the role of rescuer. Both were part of a diffuse railing at the world, cajoling and appealing. The therapist's responses each time referred to facts (not to feelings or fantasies, as one would be more likely to do in existential or analytic work) and turned down the profferred role of rescuer. In behaviorist terms the therapist was attempting to extinguish, or at least not reinforce, the response "I will rescue you, and also infantilize you.")

Put more broadly, the patient was saying "Why isn't there an absolute, dependable, true love" (perhaps the all-good breast)? The therapist did not want to make the request explicit, which would probably humiliate the patient and be denied. The patient can much more safely and comfortably arrive at that realization by himself, not feeling it as an accusation by the therapist. The latter only wants to remove himself from the part assigned of being that all-good breast. The removal, however, as I have indicated before, is also a moving of the projection onto a relatively neutral screen before therapist and patient. The double statement illustrated earlier refers then, we can say, to both good and bad breast, now side by side. This can be a step toward their re-fusion (in object relations terms), toward a view of the world as discontinuous, random, good-and-bad, neither triumph nor disaster (in more existential ones).

In short, great expectations and disappointments are surfaced, displaced and externalized, reconstructed in detail, and, hopefully, fused again. What was internal and split becomes external and joined.

## GAINING PERSPECTIVE ON THERAPIST AND THERAPY

More than other therapists, participant observers work outside the patient-therapist relationship. Interviewer and interviewee, to use Sullivan's terms, do not talk to each other so much as about others. And although termination invites a turning toward each other, if only to exchange the fact of parting, in principle participant observation makes possible a meeting that does not occur head-on. Both therapist and patient can themselves be counterprojected and separate from one another out there.

Here is an illustrative sequence:

TH: No doubt therapy is bound to disappoint expectations. (Note the use of "therapy" instead of the third-person singular "therapist" or the most self-referential, first person singular "I." In this way one achieves some of the distance public figures gain by referring to themselves as "he" or by their names.)

PT: Actually we accomplished more than I remember expecting. (PT turns toward TH. PT tempts TH to enjoy a *My Fair Lady* exchange: "You did it," "No, you did it. How grand we both are." This could be useful existentially, if it increased the parties' capacity to bear joy and closeness. It would not be useful if it were merely an exchange. In the following, TH develops what each in fact did contribute to the successes and failures of their work. This exploration of the facts again limits the projections, not reinforcing the power of the internal objects.)

TH: Being a patient puts a person down at first. (PT's experience of patienthood will now be explored "out there." Note how quickly the exploration of being a therapist follows, since the two are mutually dependent: one is always a therapist to this or that patient and vice versa.)

PT: You were condescending. (Again PT moves the discussion back into the medium between them both.)

TH: There was that time I told you how well I had done with an even more difficult patient. (Even though the pronouns *I* and *you* are used, this is counterprojective: the condescension is explored in the past and the implication is "I would not be like that now.")

PT: Is that what you meant? (Again back in the medium, although not deeply, as this question is largely rhetorical.)

TH: In those days you maintained a kindly confusion. (PT is now invited to review how *he* was.)

PT: I got lost coming to the office once after you had confused an appointment.

TH: Patients or children are not supposed to improve on their elders. (This can be understood as an effort at insight-giving, but it is also counterprojective: TH is not protecting his rights of senior superiority.)

PT: My father was easily threatened. (This may be an unconscious trap. If TH is easily threatened, he may seize on his superiority to PT's father and end up acting just like him! So, TH puts the whole set of possibilities "out there.")

TH: You've seen that happen here often enough. (This invites a reconciliation with father's weaknesses as well as a comparison of therapist and father. Such are also the impacts of John M. Murray's "we're all god's children.")

PT: Actually I never thought of you as vulnerable at all. (A nice projection, apparently little touched even after three years. No doubt TH has worked hard to maintain it. Now is the chance to throw this mask out before them.)

TH: Therapists will be therapists. (Perhaps too facile, but at least unmistakedly distancing himself from the therapeutic role. The implication is: therapists may need to be invulnerable but I'm more than a therapist.)

PT: Maybe I did hurt you. (PT is very quick to take this next step.)

TH: How could a patient matter! (Put rhetorically. This is meant to disengage the patient from his role in therapy. The implication is: you are more than a patient and therefore can hurt me. Note how difficult it would be to say this directly: on the conscious level it is too obvious to need saying and would be condescending. Yet it is an important facet of the therapist-patient relationship.)

PT: Laughs. Maybe I did hurt you.

TH: There may not be much chance I could forgive you. (This states a possible fearful expectation of PT's directly. Such statements as a rule are reassuring in a way direct reassurance seldom is. Contrast this statement with: "Don't worry, I forgive you." The "not" in such statements often goes unheard (perhaps because negations are weak or absent in the unconscious) and the sentence is felt as, "Worry that I forgive you," or the negative is displaced and the sentence reads, "Worry, I don't forgive you."

The statement made should be uttered sarcastically. Then it will matter little if the "not" is displaced here too. Sarcasm serves to deride the projection.)

PT: Once I thought of imitating your mannerisms. (Since PT says the thought occurred once and was not acted on, there is still the implication that PT felt TH would be offended. This is tricky because TH probably would have been offended. How to deal with a projection that is also a truth? A psychoanalyst could interpret the projection in terms of childhood remnants, ignoring the truth. Existentialists could close with the feelings. But all along I have insisted that interpersonal method has a special investment in the veridical truth. Therefore it is not to be ignored. The difficulty is that the truth supports the projection.)

TH: Maybe I need to get over my sensitivities. (Here PT's projection is thrown against TH's *future;* then perhaps PT's fears will not be so well grounded. As for the past and probably the present, PT's fears are acknowledged. A further bit of work may have been done: TH may have counterprojected any idea PT has that growing must stop when treatment stops.)

Participant observation means to shape the forces active in the therapeutic relationship; it is, in Bibring's terms, manipulative. Surely therapists, and patients too, must tire of this fencing. Perhaps they want to meet as human beings, existentially, or examine the material between them in the therapeutic alliance, psychoanalytically. Otherwise will not patients feel played with, however expertly?

I think they must. Before participant observation is abandoned for this reason alone, however, we need to ask ourselves whether this very manipulativeness and expertness is not the most honest stance for any therapist to take. Can any therapeutic procedure escape the same charge? Is not some degree of manipulativeness part of every technical procedure? Perhaps the expertness is best made explicit and hopefully accepted. It is at termination that this point is most easily made. Then the existential patient must ask: if all this humanness and being together has been real, why terminate at all? Why not become what therapist and patient have almost been, friends? Existential therapists must otherwise appear insincere, because feelings cannot be turned on and off in response to technical demands. At least the interpersonalist has been only the technician from the start.

Meanwhile psychoanalysts, being more neutral and anonymous than the others, have not promised friendship and made termination difficult for this reason. The difficulty of analytic termination enters from a different direction. How to say goodbye to someone hardly known? It must be like parting almost before saying hello. Moreover the very power of anonymity to evoke fantasies cannot be easily turned off. Surely the less is known of the analyst the more future fantasies will spring up.

Of course, each of the great schools modifies its procedures in practice—partly to answer these objections. Existential patients must be weaned of their closeness; analysts commonly make themselves better known as the work concludes. Indeed some of the technical suggestions put forward here may be useful to analysts wishing to make themselves known while still preserving some distance, and to existential workers who wish to gain some distance while still being with their patients. The participant observer stands midway between existential closeness and analytic distance and may be pressed into the service of either camp. Many occasions arise when each of the schools needs the others.

# NINE

# The Theories of Practice

THIS IS A BOOK about practice and an art—Sullivanism in action. We cannot discuss sound practice, however, without establishing principles, and we cannot establish valid principles without relating them to the field as a whole. Today psychotherapy lacks any conceptual framework that would permit communication among the schools, and perhaps most important, it lacks the conceptual tools for comparing one method with another. We do not know what works when because we do not know what is occurring when. No general theory of psychological work will come from this book. But the presentation of any one method invites generalizations with respect to all the others.

It seems to me that the tools, the ways of working outlined here rest on four principles sharply separable from those underlying the other best-known ways of doing psychiatric and psychological work. It is therefore possible to clarify by contrast the various theories of practice.

*First*, interpersonal work is directed at the "other people" in the room, what I have called the social unconscious permeating human transactions. Until the medium of communication is cleansed of its distorting images, it is assumed that no reliable exchanges can take place.

Psychoanalysis, in contrast, incubates the distorting images. These in their fully developed form, the transference neurosis, constitute the lesion to be treated. The partly detached, neutral presence of the analyst invites the transference neurosis which, it is assumed, can then be dealt with interpretively.

Existential workers, in further contrast, neither offer themselves as screens, like analysts, nor attempt to move the distortions away to be examined elsewhere. By being where the patients are, they assume they offer no target for transference. Inside the patient, as it were, they look out at the patient's world.

In medical psychology, finally, and some psychoanalysis, doctor and patient form a cooperative alliance to examine and deal with the distortions. This point of view takes for granted that doctor and patient can be objective, that there is some part of the mental life of both doctor and patient untouched by the distorting introjects.

*Second*, interpersonal work assumes that the other people in the room make the patient anxious and can only be removed by indirect means. These means I have called playing the transference. The principal device is talking about the introjects, thereby placing them on the narrative screen. Once away from the medium, they provoke less anxiety and fewer defensive operations.

Psychoanalysis, in contrast, requires that the patient bear considerable anxiety. To reduce it prematurely would be to abort transference development. With transference development come the patient's characteristic ego processes, which are to be analyzed, too.

In existential work anxiety is shared with the therapist. Existential therapists, being with their patients, help bear the anxiety, as well as other feelings. The defenses against feeling are replaced by the newly identified-with capacity to bear feelings, it is hoped.

In medical psychology (what I have called elsewhere objective-descriptive psychiatry), anxiety is reduced by medication and reassurance. In behavior therapy, it may be reduced by gradual exposures to whatever is frightening, with or without other anti-anxiety measures.

*Third,* according to interpersonal theory, the presence of the other people in the room and the anxious responses to them have been learned. Introjects have rubbed off, as it were, from reality; the patient's projections are assumed to reflect the patient's experience. People, in short, drive each other mad.

Psychoanalysis, in contrast, assumes the presence of instincts in conflict with each other or with psychic structures. The results of these conflicts are projected. These projections are fantasies that may reflect more of wishes and their counterforces than they do of the patient's actual experience. As a result, psychoanalysts are in danger of seeing everything as fantasy just as interpersonalists fall victim to blaming everything on reality.

Existentialists, in turn, are less likely to judge either the patient or the world. The two are to be helped bear one another. Therefore existentialists are in danger of accepting what needs to be changed.

The medical psychologists, in turn, when they are biologists, locate the lesions in the body and attempt to correct that. When they are educators, hypnotists, or behaviorists, they work on the mind. They fall victim to authoritarian manipulation and coercion.

*Fourth,* as long as the patient lives with the old anxiety-provoking projections, his or her behavior must remain the same. As soon as the medium between the patient and other is cleared and the past reconstructed, the behavior can change. Interpersonalists assume that in the absence of continued reinforcement old patterns will change.

Psychoanalysts, in contrast, regard social misperceptions as a product of internal conflict. Until the conflicts are resolved and the resulting fantasies dissipated, behavior cannot change. Psychoanalysts assume that surfacing and interpreting the fantasies, conflicting forces, and accompanying behavior will change them all.

Existential psychiatrists do not want to change the patients. Expressing unconditional positive regard and being with one another, therapists and patients may or may not change.

Finally, medical psychologists diagnose and treat. The behaviorists among them do not speak of perception and behavior, but of stimulus and response. They assume that changing the stimulus received need not change the response; the response itself must be altered.

Thus the great schools direct themselves at different targets: what occurs between people, what occurs within individuals, or the body and its behavior. Without seeing clearly how it can be built, one imagines a psychiatry ready to do battle on all or any of these fronts.

# An Instrumental View of Psychoanalysis and Psychotherapy

*To my mind, one should not substitute oneself
for the past, one has merely to add a new link.*
—Paul Cezanne

We may say that it was Freud who raised psychiatric techniques of examination to the level of a technique in the truly medical sense of the word. In the pre-Freudian era, the psychiatric "auscultation" and "percussion" of the neurotic patient was, as it were, performed through the patient's shirt, in that all direct contact with personally erotic and sexual themes was avoided. Only when the physician was able to make himself into a complete physician, to include within the sphere of the examination his total person and the sympathetic, antipathetic, and sexual forces directed toward him by the patient, only then could he create between patient and doctor an atmosphere of personal distance and, at the same time, of medical cleanliness, discipline, and correctness. It was this atmosphere that was able to raise psychiatric technique to the level of general medicine.[1] (Binswanger, p. 357)

This technique, especially as it came to be defined in Freud's Vol. XII technical papers, fell under attack from two principal directions. The first of these was itself partly the work of Binswanger, whose words I have just quoted; others closer to the

1. An earlier version of this paper was presented at the Boston Psychoanalytic Society and Institute, April 23, 1975. I am indebted to Dr. Thomas G. Gutheil for his much-needed help with the final manuscript.

psychoanalytic movement include Ferenczi (1926) and, on the contemporary scene, Greenson and Kohut. The second attack came from a quite different quarter, was led by such figures as Alexander, Sullivan, and Kernberg, and had a different purpose. While we can say that the purpose of the first attack was to modify the objectivity or detachment of analytic technique, the purpose of the second was to offset the alleged subjectivity of the analytic situation. The first group of workers asserted: if therapists draw back, many patients will be unable to attach feelings to them. The second group asserted: if therapists draw back, the feelings many patients, especially borderline or psychotic patients, attach will be overwhelming, unmanageable. Both developments had strong elements within psychoanalysis itself as well as outside it. Both could also be seen as polar points reflecting temperamental differences among the personalities of the therapists.

I want to suggest that, despite often sharp differences, both developments have in common an instrumental view of psychoanalysis, that is, each has explored and refined instruments usable in psychoanalysis while remaining faithful to its goal— the incubation and working through of the transference neurosis. It is the goal of the work that principally defines the instrumental view, in contrast to those who define psychoanalysis in terms of the classical method and see divergences as parameters.

In essence, I will suggest that the first set of suggestions is useful for the development of a *sufficient* transference neurosis (in the case of those whose feelings need to be mobilized away from the self, for example narcissistic characters), the second for the prevention of an *overwhelming* transference (as with paranoid and dependent patients). In both cases, the early attempts to deal with these problems imposed such barriers to the central purpose of psychoanalysis that neither could be accepted into the main body of technique. Since then developments have occurred in both of the original movements, making them more compatible with psychoanalytic work; these developments are specifically (1) clarification of empathy and its separation from sympathy and other gratifying measures, and (2) replacement of role-playing (a la Alexander) by counter-role-playing measures that one can relate to the work of Sullivan.[2]

## EXISTENTIAL METHOD: TOWARD THE DEVELOPMENT OF A SUFFICIENT TRANSFERENCE NEUROSIS

Under this heading I want to make two points not yet clear enough from the writings of Greenson (1967) and Kohut (1971). First: that the group of technical suggestions contributed by Greenson, Kohut, and the existential workers have in common a radical empathic stance, what the existentialists call *being* or *being with*. Second, that this radical empathic stance can be separated from gratifying or indulging the patient. This last has important implications for transference development.

Greenson provides a good starting point.

> The analyst's initial reactions to the patient's productions should be one of receptivity even if it requires some credulity to do so. Only in this way can one give full consideration to the patient's material. It is better to be deceived going along with the patient's productions than to reject them prematurely as false. The ability to suspend judgment even to the point of gullibility makes it possible to empathize with the patient, which may eventually lead to an understanding of the underlying motives. (Greenson, p. 381).

Here are descriptive phrases from the Kohut group:

> When my empathy was not perfect (Forman, 1974, p. 28)

> Without any consistent understanding of this the patient's fear of wishing to merge with the analyst will be maintained indefinitely as a resistance. (Forman p. 21)

2. An occasional worker uses technical measures that are in the tradition of both, for example Schmideberg (1959), Langs (1973), and Giovacchini (1975).

analysts' occasional failure to achieve immediately a correct empathic understanding. (Kohut, p. 110)

full empathic resonance with the archaic materials. (Kohut, p. 148)

[the analyst] must remain positively involved with the patient's narcissistic world in creative perceptivity since many of the patient's experiences, because of their preverbal nature, must be reconstructed, at least in approximation, before the patient is able to recall analogous later memories and can connect the current experiences with those of the past. (Kohut p. 148)

The purpose of this therapeutic stance is to make possible the development of a transference neurosis in patients not otherwise mobilizing feelings toward the therapist.

The comparable existential advice involves what I have termed elsewhere translations and extensions (Havens, 1974, 1976). In existential work the therapist restricts himself largely to statements that translate what he believes the patient's feeling states to be (this is similar to Greenson's "going along with the patient's productions"), and other statements that extend the therapist's being with the patient (this is similar to what Kohut calls "creative perceptivity" and "reconstructing"). Extensions characteristically use the phenomenological categories of inner experience, temporal, spatial, chromatic, and causal. Such remarks would include "perhaps you have *always* felt that way" or "you feel that way at home, but also *everywhere*."

I believe that all these technical suggestions have in common an effort to place the therapist where the patient is, whether we use this existential language, Greeson's "going along with," Kohut's "full empathic resonance," or for that matter Rogers' (1951) "centering on the client" and Buber's (1957) "imagining the real."

We can hypothesize that by placing the therapist so close to the patient—psychologically speaking—the transfer of feelings to the therapist is facilitated (hence: toward the development of a sufficient transference neurosis). Furthermore, being with the patient removes the therapist as a separate object to receive or gratify the patient's feelings. This meets the principal objection that Greenson himself makes to his own suggestion.

Greenson quotes Freud:

> . . . the experiment of letting oneself go a little way in tender feelings for the patient is not altogether without danger. Our control over ourselves is not so complete that we may not suddenly one day go further than we had intended. (Greenson, p. 164)

Greenson does not separate this "letting oneself go" from being with the patient. Thus, although he repeatedly emphasizes that "going along with the patient" (this "receptivity," even "gullibility") are all in the service of developing a working alliance, he sees these measures as "basically antithetical" to those favoring a transference neurosis. "Going along with" is a parameter sometimes necessary but always making difficulties for the analysis itself, he contends.

Analytic abstinence is fundamental to transference development and contradicted by gratification. What I want to do now is to describe what we can call existential abstinence, which stands in equally sharp contrast to gratifying or indulging the patient.

Being with the patient does not involve "letting oneself go a little way in tender feelings for the patient." It is not the therapist's feelings that are to be expressed but the patient's. Gratifying implies a transaction between two separate individuals who exchange their feelings; insofar as the therapist is able to be where the other is, that separateness disappears. (In practice, of course one may not achieve that disappearance; one may only

come close, and in that, gratify the patient's wish for closeness.)[3]

Being with the patient demands putting aside all one's expectations, wishes, ideas, and hopes, the so-called phenomenological
reduction (Havens, 1972). The fundamental rule of existential
work is simply being and staying, not explaining, advising,
interpreting, acting. Even the therapist's expression of his own
feelings (insofar as they are not also the patient's) is forbidden
except within the closely circumscribed confrontations
(Havens, 1972). The power of existential measures to hold patients in such ungratifying situations is one source of their usefulness in analysis (an overdramatic comparison could be made
with the power of existential ideas to make concentration camp
life bearable). This is the first of two principal technical points
that Kohut makes. The other is that only by a radically empathic stance can libido be coaxed away from the narcissistic
individual. Or to use other language of Kohut's, the narcissistic
patient's need to merge will serve as a resistance until it is accepted (thus we should speak here of a therapeutic union, not
alliance) and later analyzed. Then the narcissistic libido can be
transformed and made ready for the transference neurosis.[4]

Existential therapists do not later step back and invite the
transference neurosis; nevertheless it may be possible, and not
antithetical, to do so, because both analysis and existential
work have at their hearts so close a restriction on the patients'
and therapists' gratification.

---

3. But what about the patient's wish to merge? Is not that gratified in the existential encounter?
Certainly the wish is accepted but it cannot be gratified because in fact no actual merger can take
place. The patient may feel understood, that someone else is where he or she is, but this is not merg-
ing, at least in its primitive sense. One advantage of existential method is that it exposes, accepts, and
makes possible a working through of the need to merge.

4. Also see Winnicott (1963): "In the course of this kind of experience there is a sufficient quantity
of being merged in with the analyst (mother) to enable the patient to live and relate without the need
for projective and introjective identificatory mechanisms."

## INTERPERSONAL METHOD: TOWARD
## THE PREVENTION OF TRANSFERENCE PSYCHOSES

A number of technical suggestions have been put forward to prevent transference psychoses and to assist transference resolution. Perhaps the best known of these is Alexander's so-called "corrective emotional experience" (that also owes much to Ferenczi). More recently, Kernberg (1968) has advocated a vigorously interpretive stance with borderline patients, to deal with their negative and often psychotic transferences. These suggestions introduce difficulties, however, that seem to me largely insurmountable. I will argue that none of these difficulties fall so heavily on the method of participant observation as they do on the others.

Here Alexander offers a convenient starting point:

> In the (analytic) formulation of the dynamics of treatment the usual tendency is to stress the repetition of the old conflict in the transference relationship—to emphasize the similarity of the old conflict situation to the transference situation. The therapeutic significance of the differences between the original conflict situation and the present therapeutic situation is often overlooked. And in just this difference lies the secret of the therapeutic value of the analytic procedure. Because the therapist's attitude is different from that of the authoritative person of the past. . . . (Alexander, 1961)

This is the "corrective emotional experience." Although widely cited and utilized, it has never been taken into the analytic theory of therapy. I believe there are several reasons for this. First, Alexander's idea explicitly introduces the therapist's attitudes into the treatment process (in the most extreme statements of Alexander's position, as therapeutic role-playing); it substitutes, in part, attitude-taking for interpretation. Second, the patient's experience with "authoritative persons of the past" is assigned a larger place in neurosis-formation than it receives in the analytic theory of instincts and conflicts. In both these respects Alexander, and even more his colleague French (1952), moved close to learning theory.

To my mind even more important, the attempt to provide a corrective emotional experience founders against the complexity of most clinical situations. To correct a past experience we need to know what it was and how the patient perceived it. It is not enough to be kind in the attempt to offset someone else's cruelty; the cruel person, too, may at first have appeared kind; we may then reinforce the patient's response. And, in any case, does the clinical situation provide a large and flexible enough stage for acting the parts necessary to combat the varied experiences of life?

In the body of this book I have indicated the ways in which counter-role-playing avoids these difficulties of role-playing.

I suspect that the concept of a corrective emotional experience appeals to those who see life in bright and contrasting colors. Then indeed one feeling may offset another. It does not seem to me, however, that such vivid contrasts are the rule in life, outside the theatre or the battlefield.

In his vigorous and schematic way, Kernberg has put forward a different set of suggestions that are also directed against transference psychoses.

> Perhaps the most striking characteristic of the transference manifestations of patients with borderline personality organization is the premature activation in the transference of very early conflict-laden object relationships in the context of ego states that are dissociated from each other. It is as if each of these ego states represents a full-fledged transference paradigm, a highly developed, regressive transference reaction within which a specific internalized object relationship is activated in the transference. This is in contrast to the more gradual unfolding of internalized object relationships as regression occurs in the typical neurotic patient. (Kernberg, p. 604)

How are these immediate, delusional, psychotic transference manifestations to be dealt with?

> The main characteristics of this proposed modification in the psychoanalytic procedure are (i) systematic elaboration of the manifest and latent negative transference without attempting to achieve full genetic reconstructions on the basis of it, followed by "deflection" of the manifest negative transference away from the therapeutic interaction through systematic examination of it in the patient's relations with others; (ii) confrontation with and interpretation of those pathological defensive operations which characterize borderline patients, as they enter the negative transference; (iii) definite structuring of the therapeutic situation with as active measures as necessary in order to block the acting out of the transference within the therapy itself (for example, by establishing limits under which the treatment is carried out, and providing strict limits to nonverbal aggression permitted in the hours); (iv) utilization of environmental structuring conditions, such as hospital, day hospital, foster homes, etc., if acting out outside of the treatment hours threatens to produce a chronically stable situation of pathological instinctual gratification. (p. 601)

Kernberg is well aware of the difficulty of confronting and interpreting under these circumstances.

> The danger of this situation is that under the influence of the expression of intense aggression by the patient, the reality aspects of the transference-countertransference situation may be such that it comes dangerously close to reconstituting the originally projected interaction between internalized self- and object-images. Under these circumstances, vicious circles may be

created in which the patient projects his aggression onto the therapist and reintrojects a severely distorted image of the therapist under the influence of the projected aggressive drive derivatives, thus perpetuating the pathological early object relationship. Heimann (1955b) has illustrated these vicious circles of projective identification and distorted reintroduction of the therapist in discussing paranoid defenses. (pp. 605-606)

He calls attention especially to how little rational ego these patients have to receive the interpretations. Indeed this is part of his definition of the borderline state. How can interpretations work in the absence of a solid therapeutic alliance?

The very fact that the therapist takes a firm stand and creates a structure within the therapeutic situation which he will not abandon tends to enable the patient to differentiate the therapist from himself and thus to undo the confusion caused by frequent "exchange" of self- and object-representation projections by the patient. Also, such a structure may effectively prevent the therapist's acting out his countertransference, especially the very damaging chronic countertransference reactions which tend to develop in intensive psychotherapy with borderline patients. (p. 608)

In short, the favorable results reported by Kernberg and the Menninger group are due both to a vigorous interpretive stance and to the structure provided within the psychotherapy and in the hospital. "I would only stress that for many patients hospitalization is indispensable . . ." (p. 609).

There is no doubt in my mind about the importance of dealing with transference. The very center of this book has been its concern with managing projections or parataxes in the treatment situation, that is, transferences. I would hypothesize, however, that the need for structure Kernberg describes was increased by the interpretive and confrontational approaches to transference and, further, that by dealing counterprojectively with the primitive transference manifestations this need for structure would have been reduced.

Interpretive and confrontational stances tend to place the therapist over against the patient. Moreover, setting limits or structure into the patient-therapist relationship invites a testing of those limits; hence the need for hospitalization or other means of control. One value of both counterprojective and existential work is their ability to place the therapist beside or with the patient and not over against him.

Kernberg himself writes of "deflection of the manifest negative transference away from the therapeutic interaction through systematic examination of it in the patient's relations with others." This resembles dealing with the projections "out there." Hopefully many of the confrontations Kernberg alludes to could also be managed "out there," along the lines suggested and with the aim of avoiding transference complications.

Today the wider use of confrontations and transference interpretations is being increasingly discussed and often recommended (Adler and Myerson, 1973; Mann, 1973). This is true despite the acknowledged dangers of these tools. There may be, however, a considerable gap between the results of using confrontations and interpretations largely alone and the results of using them together with other, perhaps slowly developed, often unmentioned clinical skills. I suspect that among these skills we could identify many that would involve the use of counterprojective and existential statements.

When all is said and done, however, the use of statements, whether existential or counterprojective, suggests a sharp break with analytic method. Surely the neutral presence of the analyst is compromised. Surely therapists are invited to intervene often prematurely, to render shallow an analytic process which is most remarkable for its patience and respect.

No one will be altogether satisfied that existential statements are merely translations, that they do not intrude a person but only heighten some aspect of the patient himself. All very well in theory, one replies, but how seldom will these interventions reflect only the patient and not some emotional need of the therapist.

As for counterprojective method, the whole purpose is only to offset the patient's projections, but in doing so will there not be ample opportunity to intrude the therapist's projections, which psychoanalysis has gone to such pains to avoid? Again in theory perhaps all is well, but what about practice?

Two sets of reflections may blunt a little the power of these criticisms.

1. The two techniques, existential and interpersonal, have in common something reminiscent of an earlier period of psycho-analytic history. Neither of these methods makes use of a thera-peutic alliance. With both, the therapist deals directly with emotive material or the unconscious projections. One does not, it could be said, work so much with the ego as through or around it, while at the same time developing fresh intrapsychic structures.

We know that the popularity of the concept of therapeutic alliance is at least partly the result of ego psychology. As ego pathology becomes more apparent, it was a natural step to seek some part of the ego—the neutral, rational, observing ego—that could provide a therapeutic foothold. Indeed, where else could one look if both id and pathological ego were themselves the targets of treatment? I believe, however, that this was a misguided solution. For how could one ever be sure that the apparently neutral, rational, observing ego was not a depen-dent or pliable part of the self, once again seeking rewards for its obedience? And as important, would it not be best to work with the unconscious forces themselves?

Plainly this is a large and controversial topic. Nevertheless, it seems to me we are in danger of falling back into the psycho-logical cul-de-sac from which Freud retrieved us when he

Appendix 169

directed attention away from Janet's formulations of strong and weak egos and toward the unconscious forces with which analysis sought to deal as directly as possible. It is true that both existential and interpersonal method can be used to reinforce the therapeutic alliance, but neither depends upon a prior therapeutic alliance for its effectiveness. This seems a great advantage, one to which analysts in particular should be attentive.

2. Finally, let me retrace another bit of psychoanalytic history, this in a still more theoretical vein.

The development of psychoanalytic method from hypnosis and headpressing to analysis of the resistances and transference neuroses was a movement toward a greater objectification of the process. The personal element could not be kept out, but it could be dealt with, through analysis of both the transference and countertransference. This was the meaning of the famous phrase, the cure through love: the patient's libido would attach itself to the analyst, thereby making a meaningful analysis possible, but in order for the analysis to be objective and scientific, the person of the analyst must be neutral, at least somewhat detached. Hence, as one aspect, the going out of sight of the patient.

Curiously, something very similar was sought by both existential and interpersonal psychiatry. Many of the existentialists suggested that only by replacing the therapist's personality with being-with-the-other (the successful phenomenological reduction) could valid results be achieved. Here was another "going out of sight of the patient," not literally, but figuratively. Of course everyone knows that the total replacement of the therapist's personality is impossible. It nevertheless remains the ideal toward which the existential steps are directed.

Similarly, by setting itself against the projections that appeared in the clinical situation, interpersonal method aimed to neutralize the therapist. Therapists could not stand still: they had to work actively to prevent the settling in of overwhelming projections. But again the goal was a true neutrality.

It seems to me there is much to both these developments that needs to be taken into the technical apparatus of psycho-analysis. And I doubt that this can be done in the form of parameters or through any auxiliary status. The claims of both existential and interpersonal psychiatry reach too close to the heart of psychoanalysis itself to be dealt with so tangentially.

# References

There is a large and growing literature on the work of Sullivan to which this list does little justice. The contributions of Patrick Mullahy and Helen Swick Perry are probably foremost but far from the only ones. Recently, for example, Hilde Bruch (Interpersonal Theory: Harry Stack Sullivan, *Operational Theories of Personality*, ed. by Arthur Burton, Ph.D.; Brunner/Mazel, Inc., New York, 1974) has summarized Sullivan's ideas as well as illuminated his working methods.

Adler, G. and Myerson, P., eds. (1973). *Confrontation in Psychotherapy*. New York: Aronson.

Alexander, F. (1961). *The Scope of Psychoanalysis, 1921-1961: Selected Papers of Franz Alexander*. New York: Basic Books.

Bateson, G., Jackson, D., Haley, J., Weakland, J. (1956). Toward a theory of schizophrenia. *Behavioral Science* 1:251-264.

Bibring, E. (1954). Psychoanalysis and the dynamic psychotherapies. *Journal of the American Psychoanalytic Association* 2:745-770.

Binswanger, L. (1963). *Being-in-the-World*. New York: Basic Books.

Bion, W. R. (1955). Group dynamics: A review. In *New Directions in Psychoanalysis*, edited by M. Klein, P. Heimann, and R. E. Money-Kyrle. London: Tavistock Publications.

Bonhoeffer, K. (1910). *Symptomatic Psychoses*. Leipzig.

Bowen, M. (1972). *Family Interaction: A Dialogue Between Family Researchers and Family Therapists*. Edited by J. Framo. New York: Springer.

Buber, M. (1957). Elements of the interhuman. *Psychiatry* 20: 105-113.

Cohen, R. A. (1947). The management of anxiety in a case of paranoid schizophrenia. *Psychiatry* 10: 143-157.

Cooper, D. (1971). *Death of the Family*. New York: Random House.

Fairbairn, R. (1956). Considerations arising out of the Schreber case. *British Journal of Medical Psychiatry* 29: 113-127.

———, R. (1963). Synopsis of an object-relations theory of personality. *International Journal of Psycho-Analysis* 44: 224.

Ferenczi, S. (1926). *Further Contributions to the Theory and Technique of Psychoanalysis*. London: Hogarth Press.

Forman, M. (1974). The case for a clearcut clinical distinction between the narcissistic personality disorders and the oedipal fixations. Presented at the Boston Psychoanalytic Society and Institute, November 20, 1974.

French, T. M. (1952). *The Integration of Behavior*. Chicago: University of Chicago Press.

Giovacchini, P. L. (1975). *Psychoanalysis of Character Disorders*. New York: Aronson.

Goffman, E. (1975). *Frame Analysis: An Essay on the Organization of Experience*. Cambridge, Mass.: Harvard University Press.

Greenson, R. (1967). *The Technique and Practice of Psychoanalysis: Vol. I*. New York: International Universities Press.

Haley, J., Hoffman, L. (1967). *Techniques of Family Therapy*. New York: Basic Books.

Havens, L. (1972). The development of existential psychiatry. *Journal of Nervous and Mental Disorders* 154(5): 309-331.

———(1973). *Approaches to the Mind: Movement of the Psychiatric Schools from Sects Toward Science*. Boston: Little, Brown.

———(1974). The existential use of the self. *American Journal of Psychiatry* 131: 1-10.

———(1976). Therapeutic rationale of existential method. *In Current Psychiatric Therapies*, edited by J. H. Masserman.

Hendrick, I. (1942). Instinct and the ego during infancy. *Psychoanalytic Quarterly* 11: 33-58.

Hill, L. (1955). *Psychotherapeutic Intervention in Schizophrenia*. Chicago: University of Chicago Press.

Johnson, A. (1969). *Experience, Affect, and Behavior*. Chicago: University of Chicago Press.

Kernberg, O. (1968). The treatment of patients with borderline personality organization. *International Journal of Psycho-Analysis* 49: 600-619.

Kohut, H. (1971). *The Analysis of the Self: A Systematic Approach to the Psychoanalytic Treatment of Narcissistic Personality Disorders.* New York: International Universities Press.

Laing, R. D. (1969). *The Self and Others.* New York: Pantheon.

Langs, R. J. (1973). *The Technique of Psychoanalytic Psychotherapy: Vol. I.* New York: Aronson.

Mann, J. (1973). *Time-Limited Psychotherapy.* Cambridge, Mass.: Harvard University Press.

Minuchin, S. (1974). *Families and Family Therapy.* Cambridge, Mass.: Harvard University Press.

Modell, A. H. (1968). *Object Love and Reality: An Introduction to a Psychoanalytic Theory of Object Relations.* New York: International Universities Press.

Mullahy, P., ed. (1952). *Contributions of Harry Stack Sullivan.* New York: Hermitage House.

Niederland, W. G. (1960). Schreber's father. *Journal of the American Psychoanalytic Association* 8: 492-499.

———(1963). Further data and memorabilia pertaining to the Schreber case. *International Journal of Psychoanalysis* 44: 201-207.

Novey, S. (1968). *Second Look: The Reconstruction of Personal History in Psychiatry and Psychoanalysis.* Baltimore: Johns Hopkins University Press.

Rapaport, D., ed., trans. (1951). *Organization and Pathology of Thought: Selected Sources.* New York: Columbia University Press.

Rogers, C. (1951). *Client-Centered Therapy.* Boston: Houghton-Mifflin.

Schatzman, M. (1973). *Soul Murder: Persecution in the Family.* New York: Random House.

Schmideberg, M. (1959). The borderline patient. *American Handbook of Psychiatry: Vol. I.* New York: Basic Books.

Searles, H. F. (1965). *Collected Papers on Schizophrenia and Related Subjects.* New York: International Universities Press.

Sullivan, H. S. (1946). *Conceptions of Modern Psychiatry.* The first William Alan White Memorial Lectures. Reprinted from *Psychiatry*, Vol. 3, no. 1, Feb., 1940, and Vol. 8, no. 2, May, 1945.

———(1947). Therapeutic investigations in schizophrenia. *Psychiatry* 10:121-125.

———(1953). *The Interpersonal Theory of Psychiatry*, edited by H. S. Perry, and M. L. Gawel. New York: W. W. Norton.

———(1954). *The Psychiatric Interview.* Edited by H. S. Perry, and M. L. Gawel. New York: W. W. Norton.

——— (1956). *Clinical Studies in Psychiatry*. Edited by H. S. Perry,
    M. L. Gawel, and M. Gibbon. New York: W. W. Norton.
Tinbergen, N. (1974). Ethology and stress diseases. *Science* 185: 20-27.
Tower, S. (1947). Management of paranoid trends in the treatment of a
    post-psychotic obsessional condition. *Psychiatry* 10: 137-141.
Winnicott, D. W. (1963). Dependence in infant-care, in child-care, and
    in the psychoanalytic setting. *Maturational Processes*, 1965.

# Index

# About the Author

Leston Havens, M.D., has been Professor of Psychiatry at Harvard Medical School since 1971. He is currently Director of Residency Training, Cambridge Hospital, Cambridge, Massachusetts. Dr. Havens has written four other books: *Approaches to the Mind*, *Making Contact*, *A Safe Place*, and *Coming to Life*, which was published in 1993.